tt
it
ın
er

Warwick Business School
University of Warwick

Fund Management: An Emotional Finance Perspective

RESEARCH FOUNDATION

OF CFA INSTITUTE

Statement of Purpose

The Research Foundation of CFA Institute is a not-for-profit organization established to promote the development and dissemination of relevant research for investment practitioners worldwide.

ISBN 978-1-934667-49-1

24 August 2012

Editorial Staff

Elizabeth Collins
Book Editor

Mary-Kate Hines
Assistant Editor

Mike Dean
Publishing Technology Specialist

Cindy Maisannes
Manager, Publications Production

Christina Hampton
Publishing Technology Specialist

Lois Carrier
Production Specialist

Biographies

David Tuckett mixes psychoanalytic clinical practice with academic work. He is visiting professor and director of the Institute of New Economic Thinking's Emotional Finance Project in the Psychoanalysis Unit within the Brain Sciences faculty at University College London (UCL). David is a fellow of the British Institute of Psychoanalysis and has won the Sigourney Award for Psychoanalysis. Formerly, he served as editor of the *International Journal of Psychoanalysis* and president of the European Psychoanalysis Federation. At the Middlesex Hospital Medical School (University of London), David introduced behavioural sciences into medical education and was later principal of the Health Education Studies Unit at the University of Cambridge. He is author of *Minding the Markets: An Emotional Finance View of Financial Instability*. David first trained in economics at King's College, Cambridge, and then undertook further training in medical sociology and psychoanalysis.

Richard J. Taffler is professor of finance and accounting at Warwick Business School, University of Warwick. He previously taught at Manchester Business School and, before that, held the Martin Currie Chair in Finance and Investment at the University of Edinburgh. An authority on behavioural finance, Richard has published more than a hundred academic and professional papers and books on such issues as stock market anomalies, fund manager performance, the sell side, financial distress, the role gambling plays in financial markets, and the impact of CEO overconfidence on corporate decisions. He is particularly interested in the insights emotional finance provides to complement traditional and behavioural finance perspectives and consults with investment houses and other financial organizations. Richard holds a BSc in economics and an MSc in operations research from the London School of Economics, a PhD in finance from City University London, and a doctor honoris causa from the University of Ghent. He is also a fellow of the Chartered Institute of Management Accountants.

Acknowledgements

The authors wish to thank all those who contributed to this book and freely gave their time and encouragement in its writing. The interviews, which constitute the main data source, were completed by David Tuckett with the help of a Leverhulme Fellowship based at University College London. We would especially like to acknowledge our fund manager respondents (who must remain anonymous) and the Research Foundation of CFA Institute, which actively supported and funded the additional work to produce this book. We are particularly grateful to Laurence B. Siegel, research director of the Research Foundation; Walter V. "Bud" Haslett, Jr., CFA, the foundation's executive director; and Arnold S. Wood, foundation trustee, for their enthusiasm for this project and openness to what many may view as new and controversial ideas in the book. Nitin Mehta, CFA, managing director for Europe, Middle East, and Africa at CFA Institute, was a fount of wisdom to us.

We also want to thank Lisa Brooks for her secretarial support, Sophie Leighton for her editing of the original manuscript, and Elizabeth Collins, editor, and Mary-Kate Hines, assistant editor, at CFA Institute for the very professional job they have done in turning our original work into a very readable book.

Finally, we would like to express our appreciation to Dr. Arman Eshraghi of the University of Edinburgh Business School for the statistical analyses of our data, on which much of Chapters 2 and 6 are based.

Contents

CE Qualified   ⟨logo⟩ CFA Institute   This publication qualifies for 5 CE credits under the guidelines
   Activity   of the CFA Institute Continuing Education Program.

Foreword

My office is crammed with books and papers—mostly academic. Some I have read twice, many once, many more skimmed, and the majority I have no hope of ever reading. Most of what I do read involves behavioral finance, which has caught the attention of the investment industry over the past decade. My initial reading in this area in the 1970s included Kahneman and Tversky's work and Chapter 12 of Keynes's *The General Theory of Employment, Interest and Money*; these pieces got me hooked on the overreaching nature of individual and group behavior and how it affects investment choices. Most of my early reading focused on psychology, social psychology, and a smattering of organizational psychology—later on neuroeconomics (brain function stuff).

One of the more insightful research projects I have seen was introduced to me several years ago: hands-on, interview work with practicing portfolio managers conducted by David Tuckett, a psychoanalyst, and Richard Taffler, a professor of finance and accounting (henceforth, T&T). The work of these two accomplished professors exposes the role that feelings play in a portfolio manager's experience with on-the-spot decision making. We all know fear, greed, and hope, but what T&T examine is the aura of excitement, anxiety, and denial that is at work in investment decisions. These emotional responses are a largely unexplored area of the day-to-day thinking and knee-jerk reactions that occur in the fast-paced, highly observed, and measured environment of the investment industry.

What is it really like to be a money manager on a day-in, day-out basis? What emotions play a critical role and under what circumstances? Are the performance successes and debacles more emotionally charged than cognitively driven? What is beneath the surface?

The originality of T&T's research *and* the consequences of their findings could play a critical role in investment decisions. If the emotional aspect of finance is overlooked, do we engage in the false denial of its existence? You be the judge.

Seldom do we grasp why it is that we make the decisions we do. Decisions cannot and do not rely solely on "the numbers" or on some contrived mechanical formulas with Greek symbols. Probability estimates, interval analysis, and surrounding statistical ingredients are the recipe for unemotional logic. But hidden motives or whims, or the pressure to "just get it done," often create the weight of investment choices. Driven by anxiety, such emotional sources carry considerable, but mostly ill-founded, influence.

I posed several questions to T&T about the book. The answers I received help illuminate why it is such a worthwhile read.

Why read this book?

Until now, most analysis of portfolio managers has ignored what is behind their everyday decisions. What they feel and experience under pressure plays with their emotions. What comes from these interviews will help readers deal more effectively with choices and, as a result, improve outcomes.

Can you be more specific? How will emotional finance lead to better decisions?

Behavioral finance explores the impact of cognitive effort (thinking) versus feelings and emotions, many of which are unconsciously experienced. Paradoxically, rather than viewing emotions as a threat to investment performance, the book shows how a true understanding of the emotions that are not directly accessible to us is vital to effective decision making.

What are some practical insights into money management that can add to returns?

Practical advice is the theme of this book. First, it is helpful to develop an awareness that investments generate an emotional ambivalence. And this ambivalence, in turn, affects associated feelings that range from love to hate. The constant stress to perform over all time periods creates a dysfunctional environment that is not conducive to reflective analysis. The book is a "how to" for dealing with conflicting demands on portfolio managers and reckoning with anxiety, and it calls for senior management recognition of the role of emotional finance and the need of an environment for more stable, less emotional choices.

I must admit that when I first heard about T&T's research, I thought that what they proposed was dubious. After reading their investigative interviews and analysis, however, I believe that T&T have done a huge service to our profession by making us consider how we make and support our choices in a highly charged business. It is an area where business motives and the client's best interest may diverge, and thus thinking more deeply about the part our emotions play is a critical ingredient to making decisions at a higher level of integrity. This book explores the reality, the drama that is played out by us, the investment community.

In the area of decision making, investors' use of and dependence on statistical expectations may be the product of their mistrust of their own qualitative judgments. We may resist the urge to do what is objectively best if our emotions lead us in a different direction, or we may be incapable of making decisions that are on the winning side in the competitive, costly arena of investment management. Especially considering that the average holding period for investments has shrunk to less than six months in recent times, emotional "insights" may lower the probability of success in such a reactionary, uptight environment.

Once made, every choice demands a believable story to support it, to vindicate our illusory sense of controlling our hectic environment. In the investment business, we have become exceptional storytellers to ensure that there is an apparent rationale supporting what may be emotionally charged behavior. We want to make our beliefs about the world true. We want to exude confidence that begets agreement. Our emotions are hard to detect but are imbedded nevertheless in the stories we tell. Like the stories in *The Twilight Zone*, our stories reveal drama, fantasy, suspense, and some would suggest, science fiction.

Despite our sophisticated storytelling, what has and always will characterize the "investment game" is uncertainty. Uncertainty is not so much mathematical risk but is rather part of the unknown that we *cannot* estimate numerically. This environment of uncertainty is a tautology of sorts. What is the fabricated logic that explains these storied, certainty-supported decisions? What requires us to be masterful storytellers? We are assumed to have asymmetrical information that can be used to battle the uncertainty so as to benefit those who rely on our investment choices: first, our clients and then, all the people to whom we report. It is to these people that we explain our choices, providing the powerful, colorful stories behind our decisions. In an inherently unstable environment, with a future that no one knows, our emotions surface as we strive to achieve our clients' investment expectations, our boss's business demands, and our personal hopes for the future. However we frame the story for these diverse masters, we must produce a believable, unambiguous thesis. We cannot be ambivalent; we must be convincing. This is the stuff of emotional finance, as I see and believe it to be.

The untold hours of fund manager interviews and psychoanalysis of those interviews that created this book have resulted in a work that will enlighten and energize you to be better at what you do. David Tuckett and Richard Taffler have taught me, as an investment veteran, why the integrity of our choices can make a big difference in understanding ourselves and, in turn, upholding our clients' faith in us as honest agents.

Arnold S. Wood
President and Chief Executive Officer, Martingale Asset Management
Member, Board of Trustees, Research Foundation of CFA Institute

1. Introduction: Everyday Experience of the Professional Investor

This book sets out to increase understanding of the real world of the fund manager. What is it like to be a fund manager? What are the situations facing these people? How do they make sense of what they do and deal with the challenges they confront? What role do their emotional responses play? What are the implications of all these issues for formulating theories about decision making in financial markets, and how can we construct a theory of money management that is close to how managers describe their experience themselves?

Drawing on the insights provided by the new discipline of *emotional finance*, we explore the day-to-day experiences of investment professionals. Emotional finance provides a new theoretical perspective in the financial domain. In contrast to both traditional finance and behavioural finance, it explicitly recognises the critical role of emotions in all thinking and experience and thus takes into account how emotions drive investment decisions and financial activity. Traditional finance theory assumes that investors are rational decision makers. Behavioural finance introduces insights from what is known about typical cognitive biases and also uses what is termed the *affect heuristic*, which is the specific quality of positiveness/negativeness felt rapidly and automatically in decision making (Slovic, Finucane, Peters, and MacGregor 2002). Emotional finance differs from behavioural finance in that it focuses on financial decision making from the perspective that the outcome of decisions cannot be known in advance. Outcomes can be guessed or imagined but never known, which necessarily stimulates emotion conceived as an ongoing and dynamic (changing) influence on thought. Emotional finance seeks to incorporate such understanding within a formal theoretical framework that has direct practical relevance to all financial market participants and is close to their personal experience.

In particular, we report the results of in-depth interviews with more than 50 fund managers in the largest international investment management firms in the main financial centres in the United States and Europe, most of whom are managing much more than US$1 billion in assets (in most cases, equities).

Interviews with individuals are rare in academic finance research. Conventional research focuses on fund managers as a class, rather than on their individual realities, and seeks to explore whether, for example, they have specific skills, whether one investment strategy is more likely to be successful than another, and whether or not the market is efficient. In consequence, although some research has addressed such issues as fund manager turnover, little or no attention has been paid directly to the daily experiences of the 'foot soldiers' of the marketplace or the ways in which they actually carry out their work.

Our interview programme in 2007 was intended to remedy this gap in research. We set out to discover how our group of managers, who are representative of their peers, carry out their jobs and think about and deal with the pressures of their work. To the best of our knowledge, this 'real world' inhabited by the professional fund manager has been largely ignored in the academic literature to date. We wished to study systematically these individuals' thoughts, fantasies, and fears and the techniques they use to cope with their experience and its stresses. What is it really like being a fund manager, given that even the underlying objectives may often be opaque at best and, at worst, in direct conflict with one another (for example, generating performance, gathering assets, and maximizing fees)? How do the managers' personal experiences of these conflicts enter into the financial equation?

Markets are aggregates of individuals. Although distinguishing individual from aggregate levels of analysis is important, our view was that continuing to treat the context in which individuals make financial decisions as a black box is unwise. Therefore, we thought it would be useful to see if any general conclusions could be drawn about the decision-making environment in which fund managers operate and how they deal with the emotions and feelings generated by the nature of their investment task.

We hope that professional investors and other readers of this book will find these observations helpful in thinking about what they do and the role they play in financial markets.

The Role of Emotions

Barring a few exceptions (such as passing references to greed and fear and more extensive discussions of loss aversion), emotions have tended to be treated, in both academic and professional circles, as dangerous signs of weakness or sources of embarrassment and anxiety in an investment manager. Cold, rational calculation is idealised. This approach contrasts with the approach widely used in modern psychology and neuroscience, which has revolutionised the accepted academic understanding of emotion and its ongoing dynamic role in human behaviour. Emotion ('gut feeling') is central to all thinking and experience and is particularly important for reliable and accurate decision making. Far from being an unfortunate hindrance, it appears to be an evolved capacity that has enabled human beings to survive because it allows fast and frugal processing of everyday sensations and accords rapid meaning and purpose to all human activity. Thoughts, feelings, and actions, in other words, are inextricably linked at both the mental and biochemical levels.[1]

In light of this evidence, attempts to treat emotionally based decisions as essentially weak or irrational are not simply outdated but are seriously misleading. When we think, we feel. Any attempt to bypass or ignore feelings is likely to lead to poor decision-making outcomes. It may, therefore, be useful to bring the feelings experienced in financial markets out into the open, discuss them frankly in an informed way, and incorporate them, where relevant, into theory and practice.

Professional investors may be forgiven for wondering what all this academic fuss is about. As our interviews revealed, professional investors know that their everyday experience is dominated by uncertainty and informational ambiguity and that investing is an inherently emotionally arousing process. As we will show, the basic situation that decision-makers face in financial markets creates conflicts that they have to manage. Many of our respondents seem to deal with this dilemma by trying to remain coldly unemotional. Such fear of emotion and intuition (or embarrassment about it) probably also reflects the way in which such issues have been treated (ignored) in the academic finance literature. This situation reflects the dominance of old ways of thinking, crude notions of psychology and emotion, and given that both academic finance and the investment profession have been so male dominated, possibly also a gender bias.

The Nature of Professional Experience

In the course of the chapters that follow, we draw attention to five recurring features of fund managers' experience highlighted by our interviews. These features are central to an understanding of their task.

First, asset managers must be exceptional. They are paid to make investments that, for a given level of risk, are expected to lead to their portfolios outperforming their benchmarks on a consistent basis. They have to do so while competing with large numbers of equally qualified and able investment professionals in similarly high-powered and well-resourced institutions, all of whom make the claim that they can outperform each other.

Second, asset managers must make decisions with incomplete information that is open to competing interpretations. They are swamped with this information, which is often conflicting, and although all managers have access to enormous computing power, such power is often to little advantage; there are usually no clear-cut decisions to be made on the basis of the mounds of data. No decision is obvious; otherwise, everyone would do the same thing and

---

[1]Overwhelming evidence indicates that brain activity in the cortex, the region of the brain where we think, continuously interacts with activity in the more primitive brain zones—the areas dealing with feeling, particularly those producing impulses to run (anxiety) or to go toward (desire). Such emotions are, of course, triggered continuously in investing. See Tuckett (2011, Chapter 3) for a much fuller description of this process.

there would be no investment opportunities. The decisions that fund managers make, therefore, are always ambivalent and based on subtly interpreting the meaning of inherently ambiguous information.

Third, asset managers know that asset valuations are determined by their own and their colleagues' perceptions of underlying value and that these beliefs are neither obvious nor easy to ascertain. Although our respondents believe that market prices can diverge from fundamental value in the short term, they all agree that price must converge to fundamental value in the long term. The problem is always that no one knows how long this will take or by how much the fundamental value will change in the meantime. The future is uncertain; it contains too many imponderables. In a significant sense, therefore, the story that prevails in the market about an asset's likely future is what determines that asset's current value.

Fourth, asset managers know that the assumptions and reasoning which bind them to their claims about the assets they hold are uncertain. They make their investment decisions on the basis of informed guesswork about the future. Each of these guesses requires them implicitly to claim that they know something about the 'true' worth of the stock that many or most others do not. In other words, they claim to hold an information advantage. But do they? Fund managers know logically that, contrary to their claims and hopes, it may turn out that others had the information advantage, that others knew something they did not or were able to interpret existing information better than they were.

Fifth, the investment relationships our asset managers have with their stocks are highly emotional in nature. They talked about *liking* and even *loving* stocks and the managements of companies that were delivering what they hoped and then *hating* them when they felt let down. They are excited in anticipation and disappointed when things do not work out. As in close personal relationships, our fund managers' feelings about their securities are strong and volatile. The capacity of such imagined and actual relationships to gratify or frustrate constantly provokes emotion.

These five dimensions of the reality of asset management are widely experienced by the fund managers with whom we spoke and, we think, will resonate with any professional reading this book. The crucial point is that asset prices fluctuate substantially according to beliefs about underlying values based on intrinsically ambiguous information and predictions concerning an uncertain future. Because finance professionals must 'fill in' incomplete information with interpretations, they cannot base their decisions on rational calculus alone. Any theory of what they do and how they do it must, therefore, take this fact into account.

In this book, we elaborate on how these five themes dominate the experience of the fund managers we studied and how they govern financial markets. We illustrate how these themes combine and create feelings of emotional conflict and have the potential to lead to problematic states of mind and dysfunctional outcomes for investors and society generally. We go on to emphasise that coping with this situation is inevitably at the heart of the investment process and that we must understand it better if we want to comprehend the job of fund managers; the challenges faced by them, their clients, and their firms; and how to manage these challenges more effectively.

Introduction to the Chapters

In Chapter 2, we describe the research method we used—the in-depth (qualitative) interview—to help us develop our ideas about the everyday experience of fund managers and our grounds for believing that the conclusions drawn are valid and accurate. We then delineate the characteristics of our sample and indicate what we asked the interviewees. Finally, to give a flavour of what happened in each interview, we introduce one of the money managers, whom we will call 'Duncan Smith'. Drawing directly on our interview material, we describe his investment philosophy, what he believes his competitive advantage to be, and how he deals with the uncertain future. Despite the uncertainties, he, of course, has to make investment judgments—repeatedly and with conviction. He has been doing so in portfolio management for nearly 20 years.

We then introduce the idea that one of the ways in which Duncan Smith is able to make decisions is by telling stories to both himself and others—weaving narratives that *feel* true and that thus support action when data are incomplete and future events difficult to predict. His stories are about the exceptional opportunities he thought he could identify in the market that would allow him to achieve superior performance. His stories seem to help him to commit to action and to make sense of what he is doing. He can also use stories to explain outcomes. Even when decisions do not work out, stories provide rationales to help motivate him to carry on. Chapter 4 develops these key ideas in detail.

Other aspects of Duncan Smith's interview are highlighted, including, as with many of our other respondents, the importance he places on his ability to assess the quality of company management, the extent to which he thinks he can trust management, and the problems he has in managing client expectations. What we see from his interview—as with most of the interviews we conducted, in fact—is a picture of a highly able and hard-working professional seeking to look after the interests of his clients and investment house in the best way possible. Importantly, he is well aware, as are virtually all our interviewees, of the underlying emotional context in which he and his team have to operate.

Chapter 3 formally introduces the core elements of the fund manager's daily experience. It focuses on the emotional conflicts that the competitive pressures create, as related by our interviewees. Specifically, we show how, despite the low correlation between short-term outperformance and the longer-term performance criteria specified by most fund management mandates, managers think clients (and the investment houses themselves) expect both. The resulting daily pressures lead to anxiety, which, whether consciously acknowledged or not, is clearly likely to be antithetical to reflective and considered investment judgment.

We also discuss in Chapter 3 the emotional ramifications of the seemingly omnipresent threat of termination and/or loss of remuneration if the fund manager underperforms. These fears seem to be unrelated to the managers' previous track records. Because of the anxieties associated with the unrealistic and often contradictory targets the fund managers believe they are required to meet, many managers tend to use their computers to monitor their performance on an almost continuous basis.

The final section of Chapter 3 describes various coping strategies adopted by our fund managers to deal with the conflicting demands. These fund managers can be considered to be in the emotional front line of the asset management industry and, as such, have to carry with them not only their own anxieties and concerns but also those of their clients, employers, and others. The ambiguities in the behaviour of the financial markets and their lack of predictability have major emotional ramifications for all market participants. The strategies the managers use include selectively interpreting information and running several portfolios so that at least some of them will perform well at a given time.

In Chapter 4, we explore what we learned from our interviews about how fund managers are able to do their jobs when (i) their jobs require them continuously to enter into relationships with assets that can easily let them down and (ii) the outcomes of their investment decisions are largely unpredictable *ex ante*. They have to develop the convictions to initiate relationships with stocks and maintain them over time. To do so, they do what human beings often do in uncertain situations where action is necessary—tell stories.

We illustrate this idea by describing some of the stories our fund managers told to support the decisions they made, both when the decisions eventually worked out and when they did not. Stories can create a sense of truth by knitting different events together and evoking emotions as a kind of glue. Their power lies in their felt plausibility rather than their factual accuracy. In the case of our traditional 'stock-pickers', we found that most of the stories managers told about their investment successes are in what Gabriel (2000) defined as an epic genre. (Gabriel, a professor of organisational behaviour, studies storytelling in business and other institutional settings.) Stories that managers hoped would work out but did not involve many of the well-known components of the tragic or tragicomic genres. Because of the way our fund managers are able to explain 'failure' with plausible stories, such failures do not appear to threaten their meta-narratives (a term we will explore further in Chapter 4) or underlying investment creeds. In fact, we suggest that through the medium of the story, our fund managers are, paradoxically, able to use adverse outcomes to help reinforce their sense of purpose and to maintain their beliefs in the validity of their investment strategies and processes.

An important implication is that in the market as a whole, fund managers, their employers, and their clients may have difficulty learning from experience. Storytelling, in the sense that we have described, is a wonderfully flexible way of explaining misfortune and managing anxiety without threatening underlying beliefs. Interestingly, our 'quant' manager respondents use stories just as the more traditional stock-pickers do. The plot, however, tends to concern how their statistical models, which were 'free of emotion', are able to take advantage of the emotional 'weaknesses' of other, more traditional investors.

Chapter 5 explores the *real* risk our fund managers face—namely, that of their investment decisions not working out. Anxieties about being wrong were continuously bubbling beneath the surface of our interviews. Our respondents are 'at risk' for making decision 'errors'. Four broad clusters of concern are highlighted.

First, our money managers have doubts about the quality of the information on which they rely and whether they might have been misled. To what extent can they trust company management not to let them down? Second, they have to deal with their anxiety about their inability, ultimately, to predict the future. They do this by believing that events can be forecast but then rationalising in hindsight why their actual forecasts turned out to be wrong. Third, they have to deal with business risk—specifically, doubts as to whether their clients will stay the course if they underperform. In addition, they believe that clients expect short-term returns irrespective of the length of the mandate and are intolerant of the fact that demanding high returns also leads to an increased probability of underperformance. Many of our fund managers deal with these issues by 'index hugging'—that is, by sharply limiting the variation of portfolio return relative to the benchmark. Finally, our respondents have to deal with their anxieties about career risk—the threat to their compensation and promotion and the potential for being fired if they perform below expectations, even if the performance is not under their control.

We conclude Chapter 5 with the idea that however useful conventional measures of risk may be for some purposes, they may play an equally important role as *pseudo-defences* against the uncomfortable emotions that accompany feeling uncertain and at risk. The concept of a pseudo-defence is explained in Chapter 5.

Chapter 6, our final chapter, draws together what we have learned from our interviews and introduces the core concepts of a new way of thinking about finance that we term 'emotional finance'. We set out ideas about the key role played by unconscious 'phantasies' (the basic components of unconscious mental life) in all human activity, and we describe two states of mind in which decisions can be made (the integrated state and the divided state). We elaborate on the other core concepts of emotional finance (emotional conflict, object relationships, 'phantastic objects', and 'groupfeel') before drawing on these ideas to analyse the emotional situation in which fund managers operate and its implications for them and their decision making.

We suggest that, at some level, fund managers, who are required to be 'exceptional' by their clients and employers, need to believe they can find exciting and idealised stocks to invest in that others may not be aware of—what we term 'phantastic objects'. They likewise have to think of *themselves* as phantastic objects and thus, in turn, are treated as if they really are by their clients and employers. These beliefs have significant consequences for asset managers, asset management firms, and the investment industry, with all parties functioning inside a divided state of mind that is united by groupfeel.

The three final sections of Chapter 6 examine

- the need to abandon what we regard as the highly misleading rational–irrational distinction in finance;

- a replacement of the (misunderstood but widely held) notion of investment activity being driven by greed, fear, and hope with a much richer and more realistic understanding of what investment professionals truly do and the emotions that drive them—namely, excitement, anxiety, and denial; and

- a call to explicitly recognise in the fund management industry the contribution the fund manager can realistically make.

2. Study and Research Method

In this chapter, we first describe the research process we adopted—the in-depth qualitative interview—and explain why. We then describe the characteristics of our respondents and present excerpts from a typical interview with one respondent, whom we call Duncan Smith. We then discuss the methods used to obtain valid conclusions from the interview data.

Interviews

Interview methods are rarely used in finance, although they are standard methodology in many other areas of the social sciences. The interview process is extensively used for various research purposes, including theory development. In our study, where the aim was to understand the common experience of being a fund manager, the interview method seemed particularly suitable. Markets are co-constructed by market participants in their day-to-day work according to the rules and processes in the markets and the way in which actors individually respond to them and to each other. We anticipated (and believe our results show) that using the individual in-depth interview with a wide variety of senior asset managers would provide a good basis for describing what happens in their environments.[2] The in-depth interview is often termed 'qualitative', but it can also include formal methods of data analysis that allow quantitative results to be obtained.

We designed our interview process to allow the interviewer to build up, over time, an understanding of the respondents' working environment and underlying feelings. This result was accomplished by synthesising a wide range of views and perceptions. All respondents were asked common questions and probed in a similar manner.

In a successful in-depth interview, the interviewee has centre stage and is provided with the opportunity to talk freely at a detailed level about real issues of concern in an appropriate way (Gaskell 2000, pp. 47–48). The interviewee's personal 'world view' is explored systematically in detailed and predefined areas, and interestingly, as the interview proceeds, the interviewee starts to 'know' what he thinks. Our final interview schedule (topic guide) is a form of a 'standardised non-schedule interview' (SNSI) (Richardson, Dohrenwend, and Klein 1965; Brown and Rutter 1966; Tuckett, Boulton, Olson, and Williams 1985).[3]

---

[2]'[The] qualitative interview provides the basic data for development of an understanding of the relations between social actors [here, fund managers] and their [work] situation. The objective is a fine-textured understanding of beliefs, attitudes, values and motivations' (Gaskell 2000, p. 39).
[3]It may be viewed online at www.palgrave.com/finance/mindingthemarkets/interviews/2-2007-Interview-Schedule.pdf.

Our SNSI interviews were conducted in a confidential setting for, normally, one to one and a half hours. The idea was to create a situation in which respondents could talk in depth in a conversational way. The interview was built around the interview topic guide for the research issues the interviewer wished to explore, and the interviewer could ask questions within the flow of the interview. The interviewer could probe statements made by the interviewee to ensure that the interviewee understood what was being asked. An audio recording was made of the interviews.

The nature of the in-depth interview provides considerable scope for participants to elaborate, cross-question, test, and explore the narratives. As in a classic detective story, the interviewer asks questions about specific instances in a precise but open way designed to indicate that detailed information is required. For example, interviewees were asked some general questions about their approach followed by a highly specific one: 'If we look at the past year, which three of your portfolio decisions have made you feel personally most satisfied?' After deciding which ones to choose, the interviewee is taken through the process in detail by such probes as 'how did you first hear about that?' 'did you talk to anyone else?' and 'how did you know that?' This process allowed the interviewee to talk in spontaneous detail and to recall things that happened. Sometimes it was difficult to move on or conclude an interview because the interviewee became so involved.

The research process started with pilot interviews, in which both authors took part, with representative senior fund managers to explore the general aims of the research. This step allowed construction of the initial interview topic guide. As the interviews progressed and the interviewer understood more about the nature of the asset manager's task, the interviewer was able to distinguish recurring features from areas that proved less central and could refine the topic guide.

In the final topic guide, the basic data requested of the fund managers included their experience, current position, background, qualifications, personal decision-making responsibility, team structure, value of the funds under management, asset turnover levels, performance benchmarks, how the fund managers are evaluated and rewarded, nature of the clients, investment strategy and characteristics of the main fund, the managers' attitudes toward the market, how they perceive their tasks, the investment approaches used, screening and evaluation methods, the time frames the managers regard as relevant, how prospective investments are identified and selected, and what the fund managers think their competitive advantages are.

The crucial part of the interview focused on specific decisions interviewees had made in the previous 12 months with which they were personally most satisfied or most dissatisfied. These decisions could be buys, sells, holds, or even sector decisions. We were particularly interested in details about the underlying investment idea—where it had come from, how it was justified, why decisions worked out or did not work out, and how the interviewee felt about them. An additional list of issues to be covered included such items as the fund managers' view of risk, their fear of being blamed if things go wrong, their degree of trust and distrust of company managers and of the information provided by company management, and the role of company visits. We also asked how often they actually look at their screens and how they feel about screen watching. The interviews were 70 minutes long on average but ranged from 40 minutes to 150 minutes.

Once complete, interviews were transcribed for analysis by the interviewer. If necessary to ensure that his conclusions were valid, other people were asked also to analyse the material. The initial purpose was to formulate the issues and ensure that enough respondents were asked about them so that the conclusions were not based on too few answers. The aim was to see the similarities in how various managers experienced and managed decision making. Analysis had to go beyond what was actually said to identify common themes. The researcher thus had to read and reread the narratives and systematically annotate and highlight portions of the material. The idea was to construct a broad picture of the model context in which managers made decisions and the mental challenges facing them as they did so.

Interviews took place during the first eight months of 2007. As it happened, the timing of the interviews proved to be opportune. Not only did the participants describe situations just prior to the subprime crash of 2008, but also, because the interviews focused on the 12 months prior to the interview, the interviewer was able to probe behaviour after the fairly large falls in world equity markets in May 2006 and February 2007, the first signs of subprime difficulties in April 2007, and the beginning of the credit crunch in August 2007.

Interviews were held with 52 fund managers working in major financial centres in the United States, United Kingdom, France, and Asia. Once transcribed, the interviews produced qualitative data that could be systematically analysed. The transcripts totalled more than 1,900 pages and were carefully checked against the original tape recordings of the interviews.

Respondents

To be interviewed for this study, a manager had to have at least 10 years of fund management experience and, in most cases, needed to personally manage more than $1 billion in funds. The original intention was to focus on 40 managers running equity funds to keep variability to a minimum. As additional opportunities for interviews arose, however, we added some hedge fund managers, quant managers, and a bond specialist. Largely drawing on the institutional contacts of one of the authors and with the assistance of CFA Institute, we used a 'snowball' approach to choose interviewees. Many interviews were arranged through the good offices of the chief investment officers or chief executive officers of the major fund management houses interested in this research. These executives nominated a number of their asset managers, those they thought would be able to provide the interviewer with a range of views. Such 'sponsorship' was helpful in establishing the pool, although the fund managers interviewed were themselves interested and helpful and clearly enjoyed the opportunity, seemingly for the first time in many cases, to talk to a sympathetic listener about what they do and the pressures under which they have to operate.

The interviewer began by introducing himself as a psychoanalyst working with a professor of finance and investment. He explained that both researchers were interested in the role emotion plays in financial markets. In every case, managers then immediately volunteered that they thought emotion was important. The interviewer also assured interviewees of complete anonymity and confidentiality, which is crucial for putting interviewees at ease. The transcripts reveal that respondents did talk frankly in this secure setting; they apparently had confidence that no information about them or any of the investment decisions they made would be discussed or published in any way that would personally identify them.[4]

In total, the 52 fund managers interviewed controlled $503 billion of assets under management. Mean fund size was almost $10 billion, with a median of $4 billion. As **Figure 2.1** indicates, although 10 managers were managing less than $1 billion, 16 (or 31%) were managing funds larger than $10 billion in size. As **Figure 2.2** shows, our respondents were also highly experienced: 10 (20%) had been managing their current funds for fewer than 3 years, 14 (28%) had been managing their funds for more than 10 years. On average, they had been working as portfolio managers for 15 years and had held the same positions for 8 years.

Figure 2.3 shows where the funds were invested. One-third (17, or 33%) were global, and 9 (or 18%) were pan-European funds. **Figure 2.4** illustrates the international nature of the interviewee sample; although slightly more than half (27, or 52%) of the respondents were based in the London international financial centre, the rest worked elsewhere. More than 20 institutional locations were represented, with one to nine managers interviewed from each office. The fact that it was possible to interview more than 50 senior, highly experienced fund managers who together controlled very large sums of money suggests that the conclusions drawn from our interviews have considerable relevance.

---

[4]For this reason, no names of respondents, their firms, their funds, or the details of their stock holdings will be found in this book. The first time the pseudonym of a person or company is mentioned, it is in quotation marks.

©2012 The Research Foundation of CFA Institute

Figure 2.1. Managers Interviewed Classified by Assets under Management
(dollars in billions; $n = 51$)

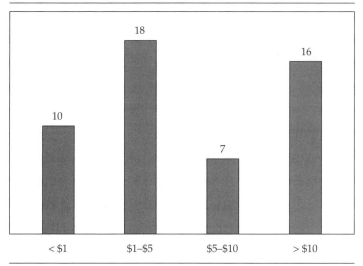

Note: One respondent was a senior market strategist who managed no funds directly.

Figure 2.2. Years Managing the Fund
($n = 51$)

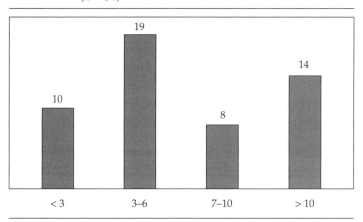

Note: One respondent was a senior market strategist who managed no funds directly.

Figure 2.3.   Investment Markets
         (n = 51)

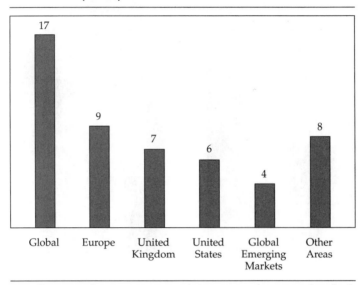

Note: One respondent was a senior market strategist who managed no funds directly.

Figure 2.4.   Respondent Locations
         (n = 52)

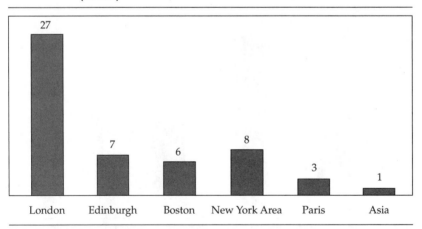

Not surprisingly, given the selection process for interviewees and their tenure in their jobs, the majority (two-thirds) of interviewed managers had outperformed their benchmarks over the previous three years, and interestingly, the exact same fraction also beat their benchmarks in the year *following* the date of their interview (see **Figure 2.5**). The mean fund three-year benchmark-adjusted return prior to the interview was 6.2% (standard deviation = 23.4%), with mean 12 month post interview return of 5.0% (standard deviation = 8.2%).[5] Because of these performance data, we recognise that our interviews may be biased toward successful fund managers. However, as we will show, this bias does not seem to have distorted the picture that emerges of the anxiety relating to potential future underperformance that these managers experience. Thirty-nine respondents (76%) were active equity managers using fundamental analysis for stock selection. Nine interviewees (17%) used quantitative approaches, and two (4%) used a combination of those methods. One traded only in bonds, and another was a highly experienced buy-side analyst. Our sample contained seven hedge fund managers and four funds with absolute return mandates.

Figure 2.5.   Number of Funds Outperforming Their Benchmarks
(n = 45)

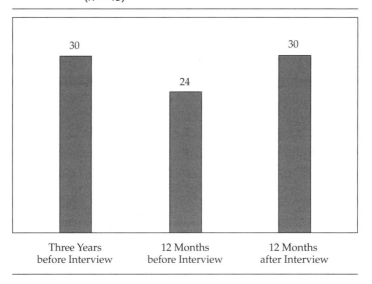

Duncan Smith

To demonstrate the quality of the data in the interview material and to introduce the world of the fund managers we interviewed, we now present a substantial excerpt from the interview conducted with 'Duncan Smith'.[6]

Duncan Smith was interviewed in late August 2007, just as the credit crisis was beginning. His interview lasted 75 minutes and covered many of the main themes addressed in this book. Smith can be characterised as a traditional stock-picker using fundamental analysis. He has been in the fund management industry for almost 30 years and personally manages around $18 billion in U.K. equities, mainly for a range of pension funds with various risk profiles. His performance benchmark is the FTSE 350 UK Index. The team he heads has 13 members, most of whom have dual fund manager/sector analyst responsibilities. Together, they manage around $40 billion in funds. Their investment universe is the FTSE 350 UK. Smith's main subjects at university were economics and math, and his sector responsibilities are pharmaceuticals, health care, and oil exploration. His team has experienced seven years of excellent performance, and in fact, the main fund for which Smith is responsible outperformed the FTSE 350 UK by 10% per year over the three years prior to his interview.

Duncan Smith's investment philosophy, or meta-narrative—a term we will explore further in Chapter 4—starts from the assumption that, in principle, the current price of a stock should reflect the information available to the market on that stock. However, building up 'a picture of what the market is expecting and where we think the market is wrong' can help to identify potential market mispricing.

How does he identify such investment opportunities? 'It's by talking to the company, talking to other companies . . . in similar industries, talking to my colleagues from overseas, who look at similar companies, and . . . taking a view on the economy.' In particular 'because of [the investment house's] size and their reputation, their access to companies is as good as anybody's'. He is also aided by a stock-selection system consisting of a number of factors that 'have been proven to be predictive of stock-price performance when you add them all together'. Importantly, Duncan Smith said he believes that this process 'takes a lot of the emotion out of it because it's just numbers and rankings'. Furthermore, he added, 'With the best will in the world, it's not easy to look at 350 companies every day, so you use the stock selection system filter to say, "Well, that one's looking interesting."' He can then talk to the stock's analyst

---

[6]Duncan Smith's interview was one of four interviews randomly selected from a larger group of interviews that were complete and that did not appear to pose any risks to confidentiality when presented almost in full. The full interview and the three others drawn on in Chapter 4 can be found at www.palgrave.com/finance/mindingthemarkets/interviews/3d-Smith-Interview-Transcript.pdf.

about it to 'get a conversation going'. 'We have daily meetings to discuss stocks and what things are changing. . . . It's a continuous process of reassessing what you hold, and why you hold it. You are looking for where things are changing for the better or for the worse . . . so it's all about relative attractiveness.'

Duncan Smith also sees his competitive advantage compared with other investment houses as keeping 'an open mind; I'll look at anything to decide where we think the market is wrong'. For example, because other investors may look at stocks through 'growth' or 'value' lenses or be constrained by the size of firms in which they can invest, he says that 'you'll get people who will filter stocks out of the universe that don't appeal to their style of investing, and I don't operate like that'. In his interview, Smith was asked about three decisions he had made in the past year that had satisfied him and a similar number that were unsuccessful. We describe two of these decisions here.

A Successful Investment. Duncan Smith talked about a company we will call 'Well-Managed Oil' and explained how he had noticed that, historically, it had regularly forecast lower earnings growth than it subsequently achieved. 'My view was that the analysts were being far too cautious in their estimates, and therefore, when the company reported its earnings, they would be pleasantly surprised and people would upgrade their estimates. So, I bought the stock before they did that and the stock went up on that news. . . . It went up 6% yesterday, and it was up a couple of percents today, and it went up the day before that.'

Asked why the analysts gave overly cautious forecasts, he said he thinks they 'follow company guidance because they don't like going out on a limb, in case they're wrong . . . [and] look daft, so . . . they always tend to lag the story . . . and that's where we can add value—by seeing where we think they're wrong'. So, to Duncan Smith, this instance is an example of how his process works best. He thought the market was being too cautious and was able to invest in Well-Managed Oil before others did.

A Company That Didn't Care. A stock that did not perform well involves a company we will call 'Outfits', in which Duncan Smith invested after meeting its managers. As with many other respondents' descriptions of investments that let them down, a sense of betrayal by management is at the heart of the interview narrative. 'I met them; I thought the story was a sound one. They're a very good sports retailer, and I thought the valuation looked fine.'

What he had not counted on was the behaviour of the man who ran the business, who, despite being a good retailer, was 'a bit of a maverick. He tends to still run it like it's his company, and it's not. . . . And I hadn't really expected that'. There were other issues too, including weather that had not been favourable to sports retailers. 'Also contributing was the fact that the company wasn't really helping analysts, in terms of people saying, "I'm not sure about the numbers," but they wouldn't talk to the analysts about them.' Creating uncertainty, Duncan Smith said, 'is the one guarantee for shares to fall. . . . If you don't know how you can value it, why should you own it?' Smith had bought the stock at the IPO at £3.00 and bought more as the price fell to £2.70. At the time of the interview, the stock was standing at £1.40. 'I've sold some, but I've still got some. But that's been a bit of a disaster, really. . . . You keep thinking, "I'll get a better chance to cut my loss."'[7]

When things did not improve, Duncan Smith felt betrayed. The final crunch point came when he realised that 'the company didn't seem to care what was happening to the share price because they weren't communicating with us, and we met the finance director and he was awful'. 'I just thought "I don't need this."' Could anything be learned? Although Smith has some kind of explanation of what had gone wrong, based on investing in a company whose founder was still the majority shareholder, he does not find any general lesson that can be drawn from the experience: '[Sometimes] the market operates in the "greater fools" area.'

Stories. In explaining why analysts had missed Well-Managed Oil, Duncan Smith described the analysts as 'lagging the story'; in fact, he used the words 'story' or 'stories' in his interview no fewer than 11 times. Like the other fund managers we interviewed, Smith creates stories to help him understand investment cases, which then enables him—both cognitively and emotionally—to commit to action. As prices go up and down, he is constantly reassessing whether the stock he is thinking about is still, as he put it, 'a valid story'. In his thought processes, he is, on one level, apparently comparing different stories or investment scenarios: Does this particular story still work, or are there better stories out there he should invest in? Smith even talked about how, when speaking to a company, he can renew his interpretation of 'the vigour of their story'. This way of thinking—recasting the investment propositions that the fund manager has to deal with every day as stories—seems to lie at the heart of what most fund managers do. We will explore this observation in more detail in Chapter 4.

There Has to Be Trust! Worries about whether he can trust company management and their figures feature prominently in Duncan Smith's interview, as in most of the others. Doubt is pervasive. Smith told a story about a company where the management was 'perfectly sound, very trustworthy' but then they discovered fraud in one of the divisions. Smith used this vignette to illustrate his concern that 'if somebody wants to pull the wool over your eyes, they can do it for quite a long time'. Smith explained his feelings this way: 'So, there is an element

---

[7]Interestingly, at the end of his interview, when Duncan was asked what the most difficult thing was about being a fund manager from the emotional point of view, he immediately commented, 'If you ask any fund manager what his or her weakest point is, I'd say it is probably selling.' The problems he was experiencing in dealing with Outfits stock illustrate this point.

of trust, but there can't be that element if the management has let you down. You don't trust them again for a long time. You don't want your fingers burnt, and . . . you think, "Well, hold on, do I really want to be dealing with these guys?"'

Meetings with Management. Is it useful to meet corporate managers? Duncan Smith views it as 'cross-checking'. Companies are not going to tell him anything they will not tell anyone else, 'so, in some ways, it's how you ask the question. . . . You're just constantly checking what they're telling you'. Smith and his colleagues are trained about the kinds of things they can ask and how to ask them, 'but at the end of the day, you're forming a view based on not just what they tell you but your experience of them, of similar companies, and of the industry. So, that's really what we do'. Judging whether you can believe and trust company managers is an important part of Smith's investment process.

Duncan Smith also finds meeting the heads of large and well-known businesses exciting: 'It is a fascinating job, and you get to meet all these guys that run the economy, basically.' Other fund managers said the same thing, and for many the human contact and opportunity to meet such people is a key part of their satisfaction with the job.

Business Risk. Duncan Smith's team runs a range of funds with various performance targets varying between 1% and 3% per year better than the index, each with associated risk parameters. All are managed with the same underlying investment process. As with many other fund managers interviewed, however, Smith's team can encounter problems in managing client expectations, which leads to *business risk*. This risk is asymmetrical: 'People [Clients] don't think of the downside, whereas we, as fund managers, have to be aware of the downside and the business risk of underperforming.' If a client wants Smith to take on more risk to earn higher returns, 'the risk is, if I underperform by 5%, you take your money away; if I outperform by 5%, well, you're pleased but I don't get any more money off you'. The more risk Smith takes on in his portfolios, the greater the business risk.

Another issue Duncan Smith raised in his interview, as did many other fund managers, is clients' obsession with short-term performance. Although generally investment managers have a three-year mandate, 'There are very few clients who don't look at the performance at least once a year. . . . So although the client wants long-term performance, they do drive you toward a short-term [perspective].' Smith believes this issue can be managed, however: 'As long as you can explain why you're doing what you're doing and why you think it will work, they're not going to sack you after three months, six months, nine months, or a year. If after a year, it's still not working, it gets harder . . . but fortunately, I haven't had to do that for quite a while.' As will be described later, being able to tell a story in these circumstances is important.

Other managers commented about their performance being public 'every day' and how this circumstance influenced their thinking. Duncan Smith hinted at the same conflict. He can view his performance on screen daily, but said, 'I try not to look at it,' adding that 'some people are obsessed by it'. In his case, 'I just look at it when I have to.'

Validity of Our Research Method

What can we conclude from such interviews as Duncan Smith's? What problems of interpretative validity remain?

As a research method, interviews have been treated with suspicion in academic finance and economics because they do not deal with hard numbers or other such 'facts' and may, it is argued, simply reflect unreliable interpretation or subjective bias on the part of respondents or researchers. Such criticism reveals a misunderstanding of both the purpose of the in-depth interview and its possibilities for leading to reliable conclusions. The research interviews reported in this book had a limited aim. The aim was not to explain *why* Smith decided the things he did or to draw conclusions about the veracity of his reasoning. Rather, the aim was to discover what common features of their decision making the fund managers would describe and to find out whether the interviews portray a relatively invariant decision-making context. If so, this common decision-making environment might influence their investment judgements in similar ways, regardless of the various ways individuals respond to it. Given that decisions to buy, hold, or sell assets are made by individual decision-makers, information about how they *collectively* perceive the situations facing them does help us understand how these 'social actors' perceive, deal with, and experience the working environment in which they operate.

One test of the insights and understanding that can be gained from these interviews, which were carried out by a trained research interviewer,[8] is whether the conclusions drawn about the decision-making context resonate with readers who have experiences similar to those of the interviewees. The quality of the data that resulted from the interviews can also be judged from the extensive quotations provided in this book, as well as in Tuckett (2011) and the supplementary materials available online.[9]

Some common objections made to interviews as a research tool can be discussed directly. One objection is that respondents may or may not actually tell the 'truth'; they may simply rationalise or tell the interviewer what they think

---

[8]David Tuckett, who designed and conducted all the interviews, is an experienced research interviewer who, as a medical sociologist, has directed or conducted several interview-based research studies.

[9]www.palgrave.com/finance/mindingthemarkets/.

©2012 The Research Foundation of CFA Institute

he wants to hear. However, in our case, successive presentations of our findings to groups of money managers suggest that they consider what we report to describe a reality familiar to them.

More importantly, as an examination of Duncan Smith's interview transcript suggests, the depth and detail requested in the interview makes it unlikely that respondents were inventing their experiences. Pilot interviews had showed us that specifying to the interviewees the level of detail at which information was required, together with providing the opportunity to probe further, created such detailed and spontaneous stories that, although some details were probably 'rounded', smoothed, or avoided, the basic picture was likely to be accurate. For even one fund manager to make up responses to the interview would require considerable thespian skills; for the entire group to create and learn a shared script seems to us far more implausible than that they were describing what they believe actually happens. The interviewer could sense efforts deliberately to mislead, or at least to provide answers the respondent thought the interviewer expected, and could gently probe a little further.

Rather than conclude that the interviews involved significant dissembling, our view is that the respondents were describing what is of intimate concern and interest to them. Because they were encouraged to talk at length, they appear to have been fairly frank with the interviewer, who, by being relaxed and putting interviewees at ease, was able to establish a relationship of trust and confidence. In fact, one of the advantages of the in-depth interview is that, compared with questionnaires, interviews encourage a rapport to develop so that interviewees think and talk about things beyond surface opinion. They are less likely to offer rationalisations. At the same time, the interviewer is able to follow up issues with further questions (Gaskell 2000, pp. 45–46).

A final issue relates to the number of interviews required. In this study, the original target was 40 interviews, but the number rose to 52 because of the enthusiastic response from the intermediaries who helped to arrange interviews. Fifty-two is a fairly large number for this type of study. Texts on interview processes usually describe how interviews with people working in a common social environment may initially appear to reflect experiences that differ and are unique to the particular individuals but as the interview process continues, themes appear. Progressively, confidence increases in the emerging understanding of the research environment being explored. At some point, additional interviews generally start to reinforce points and thoughts expressed in earlier interviews, a situation known as 'meaning saturation'. Conventionally, meaning saturation occurs after 15–25 interviews (Gaskell 2000, p. 43). We are reasonably confident, therefore, that more interviews would not have changed our findings. Our wide-ranging interviews and the extensive illustrations, examples, and ideas expressed provide a rich set of data to help us develop a theoretical understanding of the nature of the fund management task and its key emotional dimensions.

In this book, we present conclusions from our interviews based on a fuller analysis reported in Tuckett (2011). In that analysis, the main conclusions were derived from analysis of the Duncan Smith interview and three other interviews (representative cases). The conclusions were then substantiated by analysis of randomly drawn examples from all the satisfied and unsatisfied decisions that respondents reported and from randomly drawn interviews.[10] This approach applies to the conclusions we report later about performance pressure and the core characteristics of 'satisfied' and 'dissatisfied' investment stories.

When our financial actors were invited to talk about their decision making, the picture they painted of their activities significantly adds to what is usually described in finance theory. For example, it elucidates how fund managers' asset valuations depend on narrative-based beliefs about what will happen in the future as well as on conventional quantitative valuation methods. It shows how fund managers tell stories to themselves and others and have to reassess the stories on the basis of other stories that come their way in the news. It also indicates that they are not starved of information and explanations but, instead, have a large number on which to draw and are able only with great difficulty to select which one to go with. Interestingly, similar narratives were used by our respondents to record decisions in the notes they kept as part of regulatory requirements and communicated to other team members and compliance departments. The accounts in these notes and our interviews about the same decisions are similar, which provides reassurance that our research process is robust for our particular research purposes.

Conclusion

In this chapter, we described and justified the research method we used—the in-depth (qualitative) interview—to help us develop an appropriate theory to explain the nature of the fund manager's task and the emotional pressures under which the manager operates. We also presented some details of the characteristics of the sample.

We then introduced a representative asset manager, Duncan Smith, and used portions of his interview to illustrate how he does his job, what he thinks about, how he makes investment decisions, and what is important to him. We drew on these responses to explore the role that investment stories play in Smith's deliberations, the risks he faces, and some of the conflicts with which he deals on a day-to-day basis.

---

[10]Analysing and presenting randomly drawn examples ensures that one or two cases do not dominate the conclusions and that the researchers have not simply cherry-picked good examples.

What we see from Duncan Smith's interview, which is supported by most of the others we conducted, is an able and hard-working professional seeking to look after the interests of both his clients and his investment house. He also seeks to the best of his ability to cope with the uncertainty of the market environment. Furthermore, we see how he believes his investment philosophy and process help him achieve his investment targets and deal with the imponderables he confronts every day. Although he has a highly credible track record, Smith clearly feels he is continually under pressure to outperform: 'Although we've suffered a wee bit recently, most of the funds are still flat to up for the year. . . . So, it's been a bit of a roller coaster the last couple of months, but generally, we're still ahead of the game.' Importantly for our purposes, Smith, like all our respondents, is fully aware of the underlying emotional context in which he and his team operate and the pressures and anxiety that seem to permeate their activities—all of which we explore in the next chapter.

3. Pressure to Perform

Duncan Smith's interview portrays an intelligent and thoughtful individual who is dedicated to what he does and clearly competent—attributes typical of most of our interviewees. Like the great majority of the fund managers interviewed, however, Smith is continuously under pressure from his clients to perform well—both in the short term and in the long term—which often places conflicting and mutually inconsistent demands on him. In this chapter, we use our interviews to explore how the respondents experience the stressful environments in which they operate. The considerable, if suppressed, unease that exists because of the conflict between short- and long-term measures of success with which they have to deal will be apparent.

The academic literature suggests it is difficult for many money managers consistently to outperform. We will describe how, despite this evidence, our respondent fund managers are nonetheless expected to do this. As we noted in Chapter 2, our respondents, on average, had beaten their benchmarks in both the three- and one-year periods prior to their interviews. Thus, they have to be considered successful. Nevertheless, they reported feeling under severe threat if they cannot continue to achieve exceptional results, and this conflict appears to have consequences.[11] We will also report that, although many of our asset managers argued that their information advantage derived from taking a long-term investment horizon, they also look at their computer screens daily, if not more frequently, to check on short-term performance. We think this behaviour demonstrates that our fund managers do not fully recognise the seriously conflicting demands they have to cope with. This failure, we suggest, can lead to seemingly dysfunctional coping behaviour that may only increase anxiety and stress. Finally, we will discuss how some of our respondents recognise this situation and try to provide a supportive and understanding institutional environment for their colleagues. In the concluding section, we summarise what the evidence tells us about the consequences of the emotional demands of the fund manager's day-to-day basic job.

Competitive Pressures

Given the volatility of asset prices, even fund managers who are highly successful over the long term can expect some fairly extensive periods of short-term underperformance in their portfolios. It also may have nothing to do with the manager's underlying skill or investment process. As our respondents well recognise, fund underperformance in the short term has little bearing on a portfolio's long-term success. For example, in a study by the Brandes Institute in February

---

[11]In fact, they were also above the industry average in tenure at their posts.

2007 (Brandes Investment Partners 2007), a large sample of actively managed U.S. large-capitalisation mutual funds was analysed over a 10-year period. The top 10% of funds outperformed the S&P 500 Index by an average of 2.5% per year. The average underperformance of these top-performing funds in any one year was almost 20%, however, and in the worst 3-year period of the 10 years, average underperformance was 8.1%. Such evidence demonstrates that efforts to judge funds' real performance on a short-term basis are, at best, highly misleading.

Montier (2007, Chapter 14) emphasised this point by generating an artificial mutual fund universe with a true alpha of 3% per year and a tracking error of 6%. He then subjected all the funds to random shocks over a 50-year simulated life and found that over the whole period, the 'best' simulated fund manager had an average annual alpha of 5.2% and the 'worst' had an alpha of 1%. In each year, however, roughly one in three earned a negative return. Over the simulation period, almost half of the fund universe experienced a three-year run of back-to-back underperformance against the benchmark. In real life, Montier commented, the way institutions work means that these 'fund managers' would most likely have been fired many times over despite the fact that, overall, the true value they added (by construction) could be considered impressive.

Outperforming in the Short Term

In-line with Montier's (2007) expectations, the fund managers we interviewed clearly feel under pressure from their clients, their investment houses, and themselves to outperform in the short term—implicitly, almost on a daily basis—as well as in the long term, as specified in most of their investment mandates. 'Mark Devreaux', who managed a large team and was responsible for investing $35 billion, made this point clearly:

> You know, we're not short-term traders, we're not trading every day, but I look at the performance every single day. Why? Because, you know, days become weeks, and weeks become months, and, you know, etcetera, etcetera, etcetera, and it's kind of, you know, you've got to make your living every day.

'David Allen', one our early interviewees, who had been managing a $1 billion international fund for the past two and half years, reflected what others said when reporting the difficulty he has in maintaining the official position of holding stocks for the long term:

> We try to focus people on more than three-year numbers because that's the time horizon we're looking out at when we're buying stocks. Unfortunately, we live in a world where you get measured on a daily basis, sometimes . . . so, yes, there's definitely a certain amount of pressure. It affects morale; it affects your sleep, a lot of things.

David is not unique. 'Dominique Lyon', who had been managing a global fund of $1.3 billion for two years before his interview, similarly commented: 'When we talk to clients, we always tell them the investment horizon is about three to five years. However, if you underperform substantially over a 12-month period, you can already be in trouble.' 'Colin Menton', an emerging markets fund manager with more than $2 billion of assets under management, had also been managing a new fund for two years. He suggested, 'As much as I like to be long term, I'm as short term and shallow as everybody else. . . . I'm bummed if my performance is bad, and I really believe in that sort of idea, you know, that you're three times more unhappy about your losses than you are [happy] about your successes.'

Tenure and Conflict

David Allen, Dominique Lyon, and Colin Menton were all managing funds that had not yet achieved the 'magic' three-year outperformance track record that is a hallmark in the industry. So, their comments may be explicable in that light. The next manager we consider, however—'Noel Sheraton', an emerging markets manager running $1.5 billion directly—is highly experienced. He had been in the industry for 21 years and was 'parachuted into' his present team five years ago with responsibility for growing the team and its assets under management. His comments underscore how 'the marketplace' is unable to accept short-term underperformance:

> Frustratingly, [the tolerance for underperformance has] gone down as years have gone by, and even your institutional clients are irritatingly short term. And the reality is that if you underperform for two consecutive years, new business will dry up very quickly, and by the end of the second year, you'll start getting some of your shorter-term clients throwing the towel in. . . . There's increasing intolerance for any period of underperformance.

Another manager to make this point was 'Ashley Crawford'. He had 20 years managing $4.5 billion of Japanese equities: 'The time horizons of institutional investors have gotten too short. . . . With some clients, it is quarterly, which is madness. . . . In a quarter, you are always just looking at micro-changes. The big picture is lost.'

'Leonard Frost'. The constant pressure not only to perform long term but also to be seen to be doing so on a short-term basis is clearly antithetical to any considered investment strategy. It can only increase fund manager anxiety and stress.[12] Leonard Frost's interview, which was one of the last in the sample that took place in August 2007, just after the start of the credit crunch, shows the fundamental conflict about performance that permeates the industry and vividly illustrates the stress created.

Leonard Frost had been a traditional stock-picker for 20 years and for the last 4 years has been heading up a team of nine people investing around $70 billion in U.K. equities. He ran about $4 billion personally in three funds, the largest of which required him to beat the FTSE All-Share Index by at least 2% per year on a consistent basis.[13] In his view, he had succeeded in outperforming for 2 out of the last 3 years and had outperformed two-thirds of the time for most of his 20 years. Although, he said, 'this year has not been good; 2005 and 2006 were brilliant.' Frost's interview reveals how he has adapted to the pressure of having to be 'exceptional' by developing a hunted cynicism, including some hostility toward those he feels have placed him in his situation. 'Most people seem to think you can outperform not just every year but every quarter or every month, but they're living in cloud cuckoo land, these people. And most managements in our industry don't have a clue either, frankly.' Such distrustful pragmatism suggests someone who considers himself a slightly resentful and lonely individual battling against the odds. This view is not uncommon in our interviews. Despite his long record of success, Frost's fear of underperformance (and of losing his job) is never far away: 'The survival rate is actually quite low.' He said that when he interviews graduates thinking of joining the firm, he asks them a blunt question: 'Why on earth do you want to go into an industry where you're almost doomed to failure even if you're good?'

How representative is this somewhat haunted picture described by Leonard Frost? One way to answer this question is simply to look at the investment mandates our respondents have. Almost all of them are required to outperform competing funds or an index, despite relatively few fund managers being able

---

[12]Institutional factors also inhibit the fund manager's capacity to use his or her skill to act on stock valuations appropriately. For example, institutional requirements on fund managers to hold a large number of investments in their portfolios rather than run concentrated portfolios of 'conviction stocks' may constrain managers' abilities to outperform (see, e.g., Cohen, Polk, and Silli 2009; Pomorski 2009). In any case, risk-averse managers have personal incentives to diversify even at the expense of performance to reduce the risk of job loss if they underperform. In addition, open-end mutual fund managers must continuously rebalance their portfolios to control for liquidity needs associated with investor inflows and outflows, which, again, inhibits their ability to beat the market (Alexander, Cici, and Gibson 2007).

[13]To place this in context, note that the Standard & Poor's Indices versus Active Funds Scorecard, Year-End 2011 (2011), or SPIVA Scorecard, showed average annualised outperformance of all domestic U.S. funds against the S&P Composite 1500 Index for the five years ending 31 December 2011 of 0.0%, −1.2% for international funds against the S&P (Global) 700 Index, and for emerging markets, −2.6% per year against the S&P/ICFI Composite Index.

to do so on a consistent basis.[14] Such potentially dysfunctional pressures are not helped by the conflicting demands clients place on fund managers, which emerged in our interviews. *These demands relate to clients'—and also investment consultants'—apparent inability to recognise that earning high returns means taking on a similar amount of risk.* 'Alistair Topp', who has been managing a $600 million global fund for 12 years, pointed out, 'A number of clients don't fundamentally understand the risk. They think they are giving us money—to beat a benchmark, sure, but also to make money in an absolute sense, and they don't realise that's not what they've asked us to do . . . there's a lot of confusion here.'

'Julian Edwards', manager of a $6 billion small-cap U.S. fund set up with a new strategy in the previous year, experiences a similar ambiguity between what he is formally expected to do and how he thinks his clients will react: 'On the mutual fund side, you know, you always have to wonder if your typical mutual fund investor doesn't understand. They need to see absolute returns, and they don't really understand benchmarks so much, so you hope that the market will do okay so that they're relatively happy, but, yeah, it's a funny thing.' He then went on to provide a personal anecdote to make his point:

> I mean, my father will call me and tell me how great a fund he has, and then I'll ask him what fund it is, and I check the benchmark and it's underperformed. 2003 was a great example of that. . . . In 2003, the small-cap markets were up something along the lines of 40% that year. But my father would call me up and tell me how he was up, you know, 32%; it was a great year. And I'd say, 'That's a terrible year; your manager added no value for you, he just detracted value.'

The multiple pressures and conflicting demands that professional fund managers operate under are clearly complex, which further increases the emotional demands made on the managers.

Stress and the Pressure to Perform

The evidence so far is that the pressure to perform and the feelings of anxiety and stress that most of our respondents have about that pressure are palpable. To explore more formally how fund managers are likely to deal with such

---

[14]Several recent studies have demonstrated, however, that a significant proportion of portfolio managers do have measurable skill (see, e.g., Kosowski, Timmermann, Wermers, and White 2006; Busse, Goyal, and Wahal 2010; Barras, Scaillet, and Wermers 2010, but contra, Fama and French 2010). Nonetheless, the professional fund manager starts with the knowledge that the index will significantly outperform the average manager over all time periods. For example, the 2011 SPIVA Scorecard showed that over the five years to the end of 2011, the S&P 500 outperformed 62% of actively managed large-cap mutual funds, the S&P MidCap 400 Index outperformed 80% of mid-cap funds, and the S&P SmallCap 600 Index outperformed 73% of small-cap funds.

pressures, we asked a subsample (the last eight interviews) questions that were more directly relevant to understanding the effects on them of potential or actual underperformance.

Seven of the eight interviewees talked openly about these effects, and their answers are similar.[15] We focus here on two typical interviews in some detail. 'Ed Morse' is clearly under performance pressure and anxious. He has been head of an emerging markets investment team for the past 19 years and manages $4 billion of funds personally. His investment house expects the team to be among the best performers in the industry, a brief he finds difficult always to achieve. He described himself as follows:

> . . . more worried about my three-year record now than I have been at any time for the last five years—relative to the indexes, not relative to the peer group because that's still holding up actually. . . . On a three-year view, I'm still comfortably upper half of the table, in spite of the thumping in the third quarter. . . . Within that, obviously, I'm losing my leadership position that I've been accustomed to . . . but in the overall scheme of things, I'm quite happy. My four-year record is still solid. My five-year record is still solid. The three-year record is still okay, but if I have another bad quarter, then I could be in danger.

Elaborating in answer to further questions, he made clear that despite his long-run achievement, he really does mean he feels in danger. 'The situation with fund managers is really that you're only as good as your last three-year record; so, you try to produce repeatable returns, and you try to produce solid records, and solid means dependable.' His anxiety is not simply theoretical; clients can and do remove their funds. 'I have an open-ended fund, and I've already had clients pull out and come back in again.'

Ed Morse emphasised the context in which asset managers work and the conflicts and pressures inevitably involved—particularly when they or clients see losses: 'The sales guys are probably the most brittle because a lot of their remuneration . . . is bonus based. So, they don't like it . . . if you're underperforming. They do ask questions: "Why are you underperforming? Do something. Fix it." is their attitude.'

'Novak Jones', who had been managing a $600 million global developed markets fund for three years before the interview, described the pressure to perform that he works under. 'The priority is actually on beating a peer group more than necessarily outperforming an underlying index . . . because the fund is open and, otherwise, people tend to take their money away.' He was asked directly how much time was realistic before his team members ought to be

---

[15]The exception in this regard is 'Brad Johnston', who works in a team managing a $4 billion global fund with a long time horizon and where the emphasis is on following the investment process, not short-term performance.

frightened of losing their jobs. Was it really true, as he said, that an individual in the industry is only as good as the last period's performance; wasn't it a bit more than that? He answered:

> It's not . . . being 'realistic'. What ideally you're trying to do is, each month and every month, outperform just a little, so that, over time, you gain a kind of positive momentum. . . . And consistency is important. And if you can just do that little bit better than the average consistently over time, then you'll rise to the top. . . . [Avoiding mistakes is] as important as [winning] because one bad one can outweigh a large number of good ones.

Of course, one wonders whether such consistent performance is really possible.

The picture of significant daily pressure on fund managers that emerges from these last two interviews supports the conclusion that Leonard Frost's experience is fairly typical.

Threat Posed by Underperformance

The fund managers quoted in the last section are expressing industry reality. If a fund manager performs below expectations, the manager faces a significant threat of reduced compensation and even termination. Farnsworth and Taylor (2006) reported how underperformance against benchmarks and peers is associated with the highest risk of dismissal, followed by a below-average customer service rating. In addition, they show that in a typical year, the fund manager's bonus makes up almost 50% of his or her take-home pay and is more often set on a subjective or discretionary basis than on an objective basis, which we expect is likely to lead to more anxiety and 'gaming' of the system. The three most important factors in determining the size of a bonus are (i) the overall success of the fund management firm, (ii) the manager's current investment performance, and (iii) the amount of new business generated. Thus, we repeat, underperformance has major financial implications for the fund manager personally.

In addition to the pressure to achieve mandated performance targets or to be consistently top-quartile on a quarterly or annual basis, the fund manager also has to cope with the omnipresent threat of business risk if the fund underperforms. *Standard & Poor's Indices Versus Active Funds Scorecard, Year-End 2011* (2011) showed that only 75% of U.S. equity mutual funds in existence in 2006 were still active in 2011, with only half maintaining the same style. In parallel, the manager's average tenure at one fund is only five years (Bogle 2008).[16]

The pressure on the fund manager to outperform in the short term for business reasons is also highlighted by the way plan sponsors hire investment managers. Sponsors chase returns, even though doing so does not necessarily deliver

---

[16]As reported in the last chapter, most of our fund managers, in comparison, had been running their current funds for eight years at the time of interview, again confirming that they were generally fairly successful.

positive excess returns subsequently. For example, using a database of almost 9,000 hiring decisions and a sample of 870 terminations, Goyal and Wahal (2008) showed how prior investment manager performance largely drives the hiring decision. Similarly, slightly more than half of investment manager firing decisions with reasons provided were the result of underperformance.

Khorana (1996) provided a parallel picture in terms of the relationship between mutual fund manager replacement and the managers' prior performance. Again, he found that the likelihood of asset manager replacement is a function of recent (short-term) underperformance. In particular, managers in the lowest-performing decile were four times more likely to be replaced than managers in the highest-performing decile. Twenty percent of all replacements occurred in January, in connection with annual reviews conducted at the end of the calendar year. Chevalier and Ellison (1999) showed that, although when funds underperform, the probability of termination increases steeply as performance worsens, the probability is fairly insensitive to actual performance when excess returns are positive. The result is that young managers, in particular, have an incentive to herd rather than take on risk to enhance returns. 'Boldness' is avoided. Firing a manager who has performed badly may reduce the resulting outflow of funds by about a half, which is an important incentive for firms to replace poorly performing managers. The authors, not surprisingly, provided some limited evidence that promotion to a larger fund is associated with positive alpha.

Not all of our fund managers felt able to be explicit about the threats to their compensation and fear of losing their jobs as a result of underperformance for a significant length of time. But such unstated fears underpinned many, if not most, of our interviews.

Screen Gazing

From our interviews, we came to understand that our fund managers feel they are expected to meet unrealistic targets, which increases the stress under which they operate. The extent to which managers keep checking how they are doing is an indication of this pressure. We asked many of them how often they monitor their performance by looking at screens or other statistical representations. Despite the fact that most of the managers are formally attempting to be long-term investors, making decisions to which they can stay committed over months and years, almost every manager seems to be aware of monthly performance variations and most of them are emotionally focused on extremely short-term variations. They know that daily, weekly, monthly, or even quarterly variations are 'noise', but their behaviour suggests that they have short-term performance constantly on their mind.

Slightly more than two-thirds of those interviewed (n = 36) gave enough information about the frequency with which they monitor the performance of their portfolios. We found that 24 (two-thirds) of these responding fund managers monitor performance at least once daily and 4 (11%) actually do it every few hours. Only 8 (22%) do not look at their screens at least daily.

We were interested in how our fund managers explain such behaviour to themselves because many of them made statements indicating they are aware that screen watching is addictive. Many seem to know it may also be an emotional roller coaster, stimulating a feeling of jittery anxiety when they are down but a high when they are up against the market. The following selections from the explanations given by traditional fund managers are illustrative:

> What we look at every day, first of all, is our performance versus our benchmark for the trailing day. So, yesterday we lost 9 bps versus our benchmark, but up to date, we're still up 77. So, we'll look at that: how we're doing versus our benchmark. ('Andrew Smith', $1 billion, U.S. large caps, checks daily)

> All day, every day, we sit in front of screens that tell us what the prices are, and basically, we've always got a pretty shrewd idea of where the portfolio is. . . . We've got systems that estimate performance on a daily basis. ('Daren Cook', $2 billion, U.K. stocks, checks hourly)

> It is very hard when share prices are falling very, very fast and the screen is all red. You know, it's very difficult to work out what's confusion and noise and what's a good opportunity. ('Chuck Bronsky', $1 billion, European market, checks daily)

> We review our performance in quite a lot of ways—daily, which is probably a bad thing. It can become very focused on short-term performance. ('Brian Anderson', $7 billion, global markets, checks daily)

> Unfortunately, one of my funds is publicly listed . . . and it's the worst thing that could have happened because I now look at my price daily. And it's, it's. . . . I don't think it has any impact on my. . . . What it could do is make me more reactive, and it could speed up my decision making, er, because I feel more under pressure or less under pressure. But I, I think I'm, I think I've avoided that so far. But it really . . . makes or breaks your day. *And therefore, I've got to stop looking at it.* [Emphasis added.] (Colin Menton, $2 billion, emerging markets, checks daily)

> Yeah, you can see it daily, and I *try* not to look at it daily, but some people are obsessed by it. . . . But really, I just look at it when I have to. (Duncan Smith, $18 billion, U.K. stocks, checks less than daily)

> Every day. I know you shouldn't. But it's important to know sometimes how your portfolio is responding to market movement and feel whatever. ('Sol Abram', $7 billion, U.K. stocks, checks daily)

Big behavioural problems with that! I only know about performance when I'm going to see a client. . . . We don't have performance meetings. ('Brad Johnston', $4 billion, global markets, checks less than daily)

Particularly interesting is that, although the quantitative managers we interviewed were clear that quantitative strategies enable them to protect their investment decisions from short-term emotional volatility and stressed how, in general, they have limited ability to intervene directly, virtually all (six out of seven) nonetheless look at their performance at least daily. Is there a tendency for the rapidly changing screen on their desks to generate a similar addictive excitement to which their more traditional investment colleagues seem to be prone? Their explanations are interesting. For example, we asked 'Jeremy Swanson' ($10 billion, global equity) what the point is of looking at his performance daily if his process allows him to change it only monthly. He replied, 'That's a fair question. I think in the spirit of understanding what risk you are taking on, you have to kind of live the performance a little bit. . . . An important part of the job is [also] communicating with clients, too, so you have to know where you are.'

Was this a rationalisation? 'Simon Reeves' ($7 billion, global growth stocks) began with a similar explanation, but in his subsequent comments, he moved beyond it:

You should be looking at it monthly at best, if not quarterly or annually. . . . and I believe that this is totally true. . . . [However], we have the issue that one of our clients gets sent a daily e-mail with performance. . . . Now, I have actually evolved my own approach to this [laughing] to the extent that when I am doing badly . . . I just don't look anymore [laughs], whereas when I am doing well, I look more frequently. . . . Having said all that, whether I look at performance or not, if my performance has been terrible, I know it; for instance, my wife can tell from my body language that I have had a bad day in the market. *I call this one of the downsides of doing this job.* [Emphasis added.]

'Julian Edwards' ($6 billion, U.S. small caps) shows a similar subtle awareness—also punctuated by laughter—of his attempts to rationalise his screen watching:

Every day. We do that, really, for two reasons. I mean, one, we should really kind of know where it is. [Laughs.] Two, it's the only way we can understand if there are particular stocks that are being adversely affected or just the opposite, so that, if we need to go and make adjustments to the portfolio, we can. . . . I will say that I no longer have portfolio performance on my computer screens anymore because you tend to look at it all the time—it's bad and inefficient—so, I have my assistants have it. [Laughs.] They'll check it in the morning . . . and report to me if there's something that I need to look at.

A working environment where the technology encourages you to follow the performance of your funds and certain individual stocks on the screen in front of you almost from moment to moment is highly seductive. But it may increase the anxiety of and pressure on fund managers. As many interviewees appear to be well aware, the risk of reading nonexistent patterns into noise or random fluctuations in prices or valuations and being distracted from a long-term focus must be high. Nonetheless, most interviewees find it extremely difficult not to get caught up in screen watching.

Signs of Unease and Conflict

Explanations for screen watching such as we have just described may sometimes have reflected embarrassment and discomfort in the form of nervous laughter, for example, and comments about not wanting to be quoted—may indicate ambivalence and internal emotional conflict about the betrayal of long-term aspiration by short-term anxiety. A possible reason is that managers not only feel the burden of their obligation to regularly achieve exceptional performance but also feel uncomfortable about a conflict. The conflict is between, on the one hand, the public strategies they are obliged to adopt (and, in full measure, attempt to implement), which include claims made about their abilities in marketing activities, and, on the other hand, what they believe, whether acknowledged consciously or not, is realistically achievable. In other words, our fund managers have to deal with the feelings that go with being in the emotional front line of the asset management industry (and its implicit denial or intolerance of uncertainty). The demands of playing this role probably do not facilitate long-term outperformance.

Coping with Conflicting Demands

To deal with the emotional ambiguities and demands these fund managers are confronted with, they apparently adopt one or more of four coping strategies. First, they find ways to rationalise their situation by selectively interpreting it. Second, they take protective measures to present their activities in a good light by smoothing their performance. Third, they reinvent what they do to maintain their confidence through difficult times so that, whatever the past, they can believe the future will be better. Fourth, they seek to educate their clients to bring client expectations in-line with what the managers believe they can deliver, or they manage their own feelings of potentially letting down clients or employers by becoming cynical or negative.

Selective Interpretation. One way to deal with contradictory ideas that cause conflicting emotions is not really to 'know' one has them.[17] In effect, individuals invest emotionally in only one part of a story that would otherwise produce a conflicting experience, or they tell stories to themselves that are so

---

[17]Psychoanalysts consider that consciousness can be 'split' so that some aspects of experience are excluded from awareness (Moore and Fine 1990, pp. 183–184).

flexible that contradictions can be glossed over. Both processes are in evidence in many of our interviews. A good example is 'Fred Bingham', who manages slightly under $1 billion of U.K. equities in a range of segregated funds for institutional clients. When asked about performance issues, Bingham is apparently able to feel less anxious and more confident by using several rationalisations and rules of thumb. For example, when he said, '[We] try to encourage people to benchmark our performance over a three-year period because anything shorter than that is at the whim of the market', he can be understood as (sensibly enough) trying to deal with client anxiety created by short-term performance volatility. He is also, however, presumably dealing with his own concerns. Similarly, when he stated, 'A benchmark is only a reference point', he made another reasonable statement, but in doing so, he prepared the ground for variations from the benchmark. He avoids the question that his clients will have to ask: 'What better measure is available?' Again, when he claimed, 'You never really get sacked for holding shares because you've been asked to, but . . . you can get sacked for holding cash when the market races away', he made another wise observation that, at the same time, deals with another set of anxieties. If he is fully invested, *he* and his clients cannot be left out if the market surges. But unspoken in this argument (and potentially a source of high anxiety) is the difficulty of market timing and predicting future market direction: When should the portfolio be fully invested, and when should it hold more cash?[18] Finally, and most significantly, when Bingham said some of his funds may go up and others down, he was noting that he hedges his bets. He does not have all his (emotional) eggs in one (fund) basket. By framing his performance across several portfolios, he promotes his chances of some doing well and so feeling satisfied at least somewhere, even if his overall performance is poor, as Bingham himself is well aware: 'We run a group of funds. . . . We haven't got just one fund and, therefore, aren't under pressure because that one fund is performing badly. At least we'll have some doing well.' In fact, having more than one egg in one's basket is common across the sample; nearly all the managers have several funds and also several benchmarks to choose from,[19]

---

[18]The difficulties of market timing in practice are well recognised in the financial literature (see, e.g., the review in Chen, Adams, and Taffler 2009).

[19]The ability to 'window-dress' performance numbers given by having a choice of benchmarks is noted, but we found no evidence in our interviews that the fund managers change their benchmarks. Sensoy (2009) showed, however, that 3 out of 10 U.S. actively managed diversified U.S. equity funds specify their benchmarks mandated by the U.S. SEC inconsistently with the fund's actual style. This misspecification is apparently an attempt to place fund performance in a favourable light to attract increased inflows.

just as the firms they work for have many fund managers from which to choose some exceptional performers for promotion.[20]

Making asset allocation a client's decision appears to be a common practice and relieves fund managers from one potential area of stress. 'Roger Sampson', who manages a $10 billion global fund, was clear about this practice in a sophisticated way: 'We are arms suppliers, right? We're giving them the tools, and there is a fiduciary responsibility between us and them, but . . . then, they need to be able to construct their portfolios.' Similar points were made by 'James Talbot' and Jeremy Swanson. According to Talbot, who manages $35 billion in European equities:

> At the end of the day, the asset allocation decision is not my decision. . . . The decision of my clients to put money in European equities—and specifically, in a value fund or growth fund—I haven't really told them to do that; that's their decision . . . I should [then] be accountable for making sure I add value at that stage.

Swanson, a manager of $10 billion in global equities, described a similar perspective:

> Our job is to deliver relative performance, so . . . I'm insulated from emotions to some degree because in truth, a couple of years of the market falling 20%, I don't really care because I am trying to deliver relative performance. . . . I might care for business reasons because our fees will be declining, but in terms of whether we have a good franchise in five years' time, all that matters is whether we can perform.

Such positions may make sense in many ways, but they have an asymmetrical emotional effect. The feelings that go with underperformance in absolute terms may be avoided; credit is generally claimed for exceptional performance.

Taking Protective Measures. Asset price volatility, and thus performance volatility, leads to alternating anxiety and excitement. In this emotional situation, it is only natural that managers take protective measures. To make exceptional returns, managers have to move away from the consensus and hold

---

[20]Jain and Wu (2000) reported how mutual funds advertise funds that have significantly beaten similar funds in the previous year, even though this performance is unrelated to future returns, and how this practice is associated with subsequent fund inflows 20% greater than those of nonadvertised funds with similar characteristics. Needless to say, this practice requires an investment house to have a large stable of funds to select from for promotion each year. Huhmann and Bhattacharyya (2005) showed how such mutual fund advertisements seek to enhance perceptions of quality and success but underinform consumers about facts relevant to making a considered fund choice.

out long enough for their strategies to work.[21] Going against the consensus, how-ever, can generate significant stress. Noel Sheraton, who manages a $1.5 billion emerging markets fund, spoke for many of our respondents when using a psychiatric term:

> I mean, the problem is that the life of a fund manager is to be naturally schizophrenic. The fact of the matter is that if you are away from the consensus, you're nervous because you're away from the consensus. If you're in the consensus, you're nervous because you're losing any chance of adding value. . . . There is never a time when I don't feel uncomfortable about pretty much everything. That's just the nature of it because when things are going well, you're worried about them going badly; when things are going badly, you're worried about how you're going to turn them round.

Similarly, several managers talked about locking in their gains once they have them and then playing safe. As Leonard Frost put it: 'There's times when we wish you could press what we call "the index key"; where you've had a really good eight months, you are up, everything's good, and you say, "Well, I want to lock that in."' Ashley Crawford made the same point:

> It depends where you are in the performance cycle as a fund manager. If you're ahead of the game, you can afford to sit on those things that haven't yet worked out. If you have had a bad year, you are more likely . . . to play safe. . . . Let's say you put on 7% over the index in nine months. There is an alarm bell that is going to ring and say, 'Well, actually, that's pretty good. We should start locking some of that in.' . . . There's no point in getting it wrong and then handing it all back because the client will be happy with what you've done that year. So, you will bank that.[22]

Reinventing the Investment Narrative. When investments fail and managers underperform, those managers are at risk. One way our interviewees cope with the risk is to reinvent themselves or their strategies while, at the same time, assuring others and perhaps even themselves that they are staying true to their investment philosophy. Most managers consider it suicidal to admit that their philosophy is not working.

---

[21]Cremers and Petajisto (2009) reported that mutual funds with stock holdings that clearly deviate from benchmark holdings (which they describe as high 'Active Share') significantly outperform the index whereas closet indexers (low 'Active Share') significantly underperform. In addition, the performance of high Active Share funds continues to persist over the following year.
[22]Kempf, Ruenzi, and Thiele (2009) demonstrated empirically that fund managers deal with poor midyear performance by either decreasing risk relative to leading managers to reduce the risk of job loss or, when employment risk is low, increasing risk in an attempt to catch up with the midyear winners.

A good example of a complete change of investment strategy that is apparently still consistent with the old investment philosophy is provided by Andrew Smith, who manages $1 billion in U.S. large caps. At the time of his interview, he had been working for his house for two and a half years, and during that time, the house's investment approach had been 'out of style'. It had responded by reorganizing the way it used its in-house financial analysts and was also in the process of moving from risk-constrained, tracking error–type managed portfolios toward 'best idea', concentrated ones. Yet, Smith insisted, it was maintaining its basic approach. (Others in the sample, interestingly, had gone in the other direction.) Smith said,

> It's been out of favour for four of the last five years. We have an investment philosophy, and if we're true to ourselves, we have to stick with our investment philosophy. . . . We tried to tweak the process a little bit, but we haven't changed our philosophy. . . . This has been a long stretch, seven years, since 2000, that it's been grossly out of favour. This year suggests that it will come back our way; the first three weeks of the year have been pretty good. [Laughter.] . . . If you change your philosophy, you've got nothing. I think we have to stick with what we do and be confident that it will find favour again.

'Alan Thomas', who runs a $1 billion central European fund, told another story about a performance hiatus. He reported that he had done well in recent times but was finding it hard to pick alternative stocks to those he held because all values in the market had been bid up. His stocks were, therefore, 'taking a break':

> Basically, the stocks that performed very well in 2006 are taking a break because they've done probably two years' worth of performance in just one. I can't sell them and take profit because I have to be in them, and I don't have new ideas to replace them; that's one thing, er, so they are taking a break.

Managing Clients: The Role of Trust. Other ways our fund managers deal with conflicts in their situations include educating their clients to have realistic expectations and altering their own expectations of their obligations to their clients. 'Warren York', who manages a large absolute return global hedge fund, said he had underperformed in only three or four quarters in the past 10 years but was nevertheless in a hole—if 'half out of it'—when interviewed. He explains such difficulties to himself and to his clients by using probability theories about 'drawing from an urn' and randomness, which he suggested 'provides comfort'—particularly because the investment house is not going to change its process whatever the pressure and 'we always come back strong in the end'.

'Paul Salisbury', who runs a $1.5 billion quantitative hedge fund, keeps a careful eye on his important clients and manages the relationship carefully:

I think [risk control] is when the difference between the various investor types shows up, so for our institutional investors, we tend to have very close, and usually very good, relationships. . . . The problem comes when we deal with intermediaries, who, in turn, have a bigger problem if they're dealing with retail investors because that dialogue cannot take place, with the result that money moves out quickly.

Fred Bingham, $500 million invested in U.K. equities, explained what he calls 'client education':

When a client becomes a client, we encourage a meeting . . . because we find, often, it goes wrong if a client is thinking, 'Well, I want him to do that', and we're thinking, 'I think he wants that.' It's interesting: We've got a client now who's come on recently, and it's client education as much as anything else because I think he wants us to be more like a trader. His background is scrap-metal trading. If he sees a profit, he says, 'Why don't you take it?' or that kind of thing. And we'd say, 'No, you can do that with your own portfolio.' It's very hard for him to get out of the trading mentality. . . . Communication is everything.

Bingham then quoted his former boss: 'My old boss, J, always said, "If it isn't working with a client, sack him before he sacks you. If you're worried about making a decision for a client, you're actually not doing him a service."' He concluded, 'So, it's a very interesting. . . . It's mutual trust between a client and us.'

Another way to manage anxiety is to be cynical—as we saw with Leonard Frost. Many such managers indicated through the tone in which they spoke that they have learned to distance themselves. In such instances, they educate themselves, so to speak, rather than their clients.

Finally, a very different approach is exemplified by 'Charlie Fraser', who runs a $9 billion Indian hedge fund. Fraser sets out to build confidence in his clients through deliberate efforts to achieve their trust, including letting them know when he thinks it might be wiser for them to avoid investment in his regionally based fund:

We try to maintain good relations with the investors in the fund. So, we try to give them a genuine view. . . . Twice in the past three years, we've gone out and told our investors to sell our fund. Both cases, call it luck or whatever . . . the market fell—17% in two days, and then last May, it was 30% in a month. It's a lot easier for us to come back to our clients and say, 'Okay, we mentioned this event; it happened; now we would look to buy [our region] again.' And partly it's building up trust; I'm trying to build up trust basically in the client base.

The role of mutual trust is clearly key in helping managers deal with their client-related anxieties.

Helping Others to Cope

A significant number of the fund managers interviewed also have managerial responsibilities. How they exercise these roles adds detail to the picture so far established of a pressurised environment. An understanding and emotionally supportive manager can play a constructive role in helping those directly in the firing line deal with the anxiety and stress inherent in their work. For example, top management can be important in alleviating the pressure for short-term performance and can facilitate a focus on long-term time horizons. Ed Morse appreciates his particular investment house's approach, which is to reduce the short-term pressures that might otherwise undermine long-term strategies. Contrasting his experience with others, he argued,

> A lot of houses will apply pressure explicitly or implicitly on individuals, and that pressure then means that everyone's horizons come in. . . . Now, I'm not trying to tell you this is Nirvana here and we don't get pressure, [but] I'd say 90% of our competitors are looking . . . at a 12-month horizon at best. . . . Look at the trading levels. Look at the turnover—high levels of turnover.

Novak Jones, $600 million in global developed markets, explained how he tries to discourage his team from monitoring their performance daily 'because I think it can lead to "short-termism", particularly in turmoil markets. I'll tell people to turn their screens off.' In fact, two weeks before his interview in mid-August 2007 (on the first day of the stock market panic), Jones sent his team home. He wanted to keep them inactive: 'I basically said at lunch time, "Right, people are just free to go. It's been a tough week; just time out."' The idea was to help his team keep a longer-term focus: 'It's all too easy to get sucked into the short-term noise in the marketplace.'

Leonard Frost also tries to help his team of seven cope with the pressures. He tries to get them to appreciate the difficulty of what they are doing by giving everyone a copy of Taleb's book (2004) on randomness in markets and tries to instil his own highly 'realistic' approach in his team. 'Taleb and all that', he said. 'On any day, you stand, if you're skilful, a 50.2% chance of performing. So, are you going to be upset half the days? I do genuinely think it detracts from your ability to make a decision sometimes.' Frost was asked directly how he deals with the difficulty of measuring performance—and thus correlating skill and outcome—in his team. He claimed to judge his managers over a long-term trading horizon: 'I always say to the guys, "You've got three years." And I'm quite honest when I recruit people: "I'm not short term; you're going to get three years." . . . Basically, in three years, you should know if someone's any good or not.' He has a somewhat resigned approach, however, to the impact of reason in the highly emotional situation in which fund managers find themselves. 'They feel the need . . . they actually sit there when they arrive in the morning, and they say, "Oh, I made 3 bps yesterday" as if there's some kind of significance to it.'

He helps team members through the experience of poor performance as follows:

> What I do if they're having a bad time is I back them far more, support them far more, try and keep their confidence up because the biggest risk of an underperforming fund manager is that they stop doing things and stop backing their judgement. . . . And the inverse—if they're having a good time, I'm probably pretty horrible to them. Because the biggest risk of somebody doing well is they get too confident, take too much risk.

> [If an individual has significantly underperformed], you begin by trying to understand where that underperformance has come from. And you try and manage it in a constructive manner, largely through the group, as opposed to a one on one. . . . It demands patience, in the sense that, I think, all fund managers know that they will go through periods of underperformance. [Pause.] And what they look for from their peers is help and tolerance . . . rather than being browbeaten.

Summary and Conclusion

In this chapter, we have explored some of the conflicting pressures fund managers operate under and the potential emotional toll this situation can take. The impact of the high levels of anxiety and stress has not been formally discussed before, to our knowledge, although this environment seems to be a necessary concomitant of fund management. We also considered various ways in which our fund manager respondents try to cope with the demands placed on them.

Specifically, we showed how, despite short-term outperformance bearing little relationship to the long-term performance criteria specified by most fund mandates, clients and the investment houses themselves seem to expect short-term outperformance. The daily pressures that ensue from this expectation lead to anxiety, whether consciously acknowledged or not, which is, of course, antithetical to reflective and considered investment management. We also pointed out the emotional ramifications of the threat of termination and/ or loss of remuneration if the fund manager underperforms, which include fear that seems unrelated to a previous track record. The anxieties associated with unrealistic (and often contradictory) targets are often reflected in addictive screen-based monitoring. We also found this behaviour in almost all the quantitative fund managers in our sample. The rationalisations provided by the respondents for this behaviour are, to our mind, exactly that.

The chapter presented some of the coping strategies our fund managers adopt in dealing with their environment. These strategies include selectively interpreting information in terms of what they want to believe and, most importantly, managing a range of funds so that some can be pointed to at any time as performing well. Also, they may 'reinvent' themselves and their strategy if things have been going badly, thus replacing anxiety with hope. Perhaps most effective, however, is the development of relationships of mutual trust with major clients. Finally, based on the evidence of our interviews, we pointed out the vital role good management and sensitive team leadership can play in dealing with the anxiety and stress that go with the territory. A psychologically attuned manager may have a significant impact in helping a team be more effective in what it does.

In the next chapter, we show how our fund manager respondents make sense of what they do and the underlying lack of predictability in their investment task and the markets.

4. Achieving Conviction by Telling Stories

The fund managers we interviewed operate in a highly competitive and emotionally demanding environment. They are required to generate exceptional investment performance in both the short and long term, and they must find ways to deal with the conflicting demands placed on them. They are swamped with an enormous amount of ambiguous information, and as could be glimpsed in the case of Duncan Smith in Chapter 2, their investment decisions may be only loosely related to subsequent outcomes.

To do their job, fund managers need to be able to enter into relationships with investments, despite the fact that the investments may let them down and, even if they do not, often take time to reach expectations. The managers must be decisive in situations of uncertainty and keep their nerve when the market is moving against them. They need to persevere without succumbing to the threat several of our respondents mentioned of 'capitulating' (i.e., selling out) for the 'wrong' reasons.

How does an asset manager arrive at the conviction necessary to make an investment decision in the first place and then keep this position open for several months, or years, often in the face of considerable adversity and with the eventual outcome uncertain? In this chapter, we describe how our fund managers deal with this key requirement of their task and suggest an aspect previously overlooked in academic finance that has major consequences for how investment managers make decisions. Creating the conviction to act is not a simple matter of overconfidence as so often supposed.[23] The strong impression we drew from our interviews is that most of our respondents are rather thoughtful and modest. It is the stories they generate that give them confidence and create belief.

We do not want to be misunderstood. We are not suggesting that our fund managers are irrational and that any old story will do. The stories they tell are about the things happening to companies, economies, countries, resources, and innovations and how they imagine, given all the information available to them, other investors would respond. In other words, they are stories about the fundamentals that, in the long run, should drive prices. Because the future is uncertain, however, how the stories will actually play out cannot be known directly or in advance.

The stories our fund managers tell about their investments play a key role in generating the confidence and assurance they require to make daily decisions in a chaotic, ambiguous, and highly unpredictable situation. As the reader

---

[23]Interestingly, little research evidence demonstrates actual overconfident behaviour by fund managers. An exception is provided by Choi and Lou (2010), although they find this bias is stronger among inexperienced managers and largely absent among experienced ones, in which category we would locate our respondents.

will see, both the traditional fund managers *and* the quantitative fund managers in our sample rely on the medium of story in similar ways. To explore this understanding in more detail, we consider first the stories our traditional fund managers told and then those of the quants about what they did. We start with 4 interviews randomly chosen from the 39 stock-pickers.[24] In particular, we examine how these four managers explain the investment decisions in the 12 months prior to their interviews with which they were most satisfied and most dissatisfied.

Let us start with 'George Monroe', who manages a $15 billion global value fund, and his investment in a U.S. restaurant chain we will call 'Fast Foods'. We asked Monroe how this investment came about. He related that he had some initial interest but 'didn't know enough as to what was going on with the name'. It was not, he thought, 'an easy company to see' through. So, he went to a company meeting to learn more: 'They had a meeting at their headquarters.' And when he met the management, he quickly formed the impression that 'they really try to focus on managing their business', and he was impressed. 'I said, "Oh, my goodness, I think I like what I'm hearing."'

Back in his office the next day, he began 'pushing the numbers . . . I came up with a number that was 10% higher than consensus street estimates', he said, and he believed 'it could go even more . . . if this new product line . . . then it's even better'. On top of these beliefs, there was an 'international kicker'—in other words, they were expanding globally. Also, George Monroe was delighted that 'they really kept talking about monitoring risk and measuring risk and getting risk out of the business model'. This approach made him feel secure: 'Now, other people don't get so excited about that, but I say, "Oh, they're taking risk away." . . . Your chance of success is so much higher.' Monroe bought the shares. 'It was great', he said, 'all of those things sort of played out in spades, like way beyond what I had imagined. . . . It's really gone up a lot, probably 50%, and they are continuing to execute just incredibly well. I think this next quarter is going to be humungous.'

As the reader will observe, George Monroe, in explaining his investment in Fast Foods, is naturally weaving a story with a beginning, middle, and end. The initial trigger is based on curiosity, and the plot involves an undervalued business that he manages uniquely to identify through his detailed analysis (the market is wrong). Then follows a successful outcome—a price increase of 50%, with more to follow. The story he constructs allows Monroe to make sense of what he did and his investment success. He experiences pride in his competence and abilities, and the story also shows him that analysis of this

---

[24]These four interviews are typical of most of our interview narratives. We concentrate on them here to avoid swamping the reader with the full panoply of investment stories (more than 200 in total), which were usually similar. Further detail is provided in note 6.

nature can identify situations that others miss. At a deeper level, Monroe can feel that the uncertain and unpredictable world he operates in can be 'managed' in this way, and he can see an underlying pattern and sense in what he does.

Of course, the information he drew on was equally available to the other fund managers at the same investment meeting. George Monroe even wondered why everyone did not leave the meeting at Fast Foods' headquarters with the same idea he had and buy the stock; Monroe actually worried that no investment opportunity would be open.

In George Monroe's interview, we can see how his ability to tell a credible story to himself gave him the necessary conviction to enter into his relationship with Fast Foods. Monroe is not alone in this process. Most of the stock-pickers we interviewed engaged in storytelling when explaining how they made investment decisions. In fact, our fund managers used the term 'story' to introduce or describe their investment decisions no less than 151 times and used the word 'stories' 20 times. On average, the term was used more than three times in each interview. Our fund managers are apparently well aware of the crucial role storytelling plays in helping them make sense of their investment task.

Stories and Plots

Telling stories is a fundamental human activity central to establishing meaning. It is so automatic and so much part of human life that the 'ways of telling and the ways of conceptualizing that go with them become so habitual that they finally become recipes for structuring experience itself' (Bruner 2004, p. 708). Our interviews revealed how our fund managers seek to make sense of their task 'by fitting [their experiences] into different cognitive schemata, linking them to earlier experiences, or placing them in plots that can be readily recognised, in short turning them into *stories*' (Gabriel 2008, p. 263).

Gabriel (2000) discussed how stories can be considered in some detail. For example, he defined them as 'narratives with plots and characters, generating emotion in narrator and audience through a poetic elaboration of *symbolic* material' [p. 239; emphasis added]. Story content may, therefore, be a product of fantasy or experience, including that of earlier narratives. The plots themselves 'entail conflicts, predicaments, trials, coincidences, and crises that call for choices, decisions, actions, and interactions, whose actual outcomes are often at odds with the characters' intentions and purposes' (Gabriel 2000, p. 239). The plot functions to transform a chronicle or sequence of events into stories— knitting them together so that we can recognise their deeper significance and interconnectedness and why they occur (Gabriel 2008, p. 195). The pattern of events George Monroe recounted in describing why he invested in Fast Foods, like Duncan Smith's accounts of Well-Managed Oil and Outfits in Chapter 2, is more than mere 'narrative'.

Stories are clearly powerful devices for managing meaning. Meaning is generated in stories through a series of identifiable mechanisms that Gabriel (2000) termed 'poetic tropes' (or themes) that function as interpretative devices to give a story its emotional power. These tropes supply explanations for events by attributing motive, causal connections, responsibility, agency, blame, credit, fate, emotion, and so forth.[25] In this way, *purpose* is typically attributed to particular events in stories, even if those events might otherwise be seen as unpredictable or accidental. This assignment of purpose is what many of our fund managers appeared to be doing when relating their successful and disappointing investment outcomes.

In his study of organisational storytelling based on 130 interviews and more than 400 distinct narratives, Gabriel (2000) identified four generic types of story. One type is the *epic*. Many of the stories our fund managers told about investments that worked out were of this nature. The plot in an epic focuses on a significant achievement, a 'noble victory', or success in a contest, challenge, or trial. Epics are designed to generate a feeling of pride in the narrator and admiration (and even envy) in the listener for the protagonist or 'hero'. They always have a happy ending. **Exhibit 4.1** summarises the characteristics in the epic story mode.

Exhibit 4.1. Two Generic Story Modes

	Epic Story	Tragic Story
Protagonist	Hero	Undeserving victim
Other characters	Rescue object, assistant, villain	Villain, supportive helper
Plot focus	Achievement, noble victory, success	Undeserved misfortune, trauma
Predicament	Contest, challenge, trial, test, mission, quest, sacrifice	Crime, accident, insult, injury, loss, mistake, repetition, misrecognition
Poetic tropes	1. Agency 2. Motive 3. Credit 4. Fixed qualities (nobility, courage, loyalty, selflessness, honour, ambition)	1. Malevolent fate 2. Blame 3. Unity 4. Motive (to the villain) 5. Fixed qualities by juxtaposition (victim: noble, decent, worthy, good; villain: evil, devious, mean)
Emotions	Pride, admiration, nostalgia, envy	Sorrow, pity, fear, anger, pathos

Source: Gabriel (2000, Table 3.1, pp. 83–84).

---

[25]See Gabriel (2000, pp. 36–42) for a more detailed discussion.

George Monroe's story about his Fine Foods success is clearly in the epic genre, with him narrating and playing the role of hero. Deconstructing the story metaphorically, we see that the plot is built around how Monroe won a noble victory in his implicit contest with other fund managers in the quest to identify undervalued stocks, which he did in a courageous way through the agency of rigorous financial analysis.[26] The story inspires emotions of pride (in the narrator) and also admiration (in the interviewer, proxying for colleagues, superiors, and clients). Importantly, the excited emotions that the success of Monroe's investment evokes—an expected 'humungous next quarter'—not only justifies his conviction to invest in Fast Foods in the first place but also reinforces his confidence in the value of his investment approach in general.

Gabriel (2000) identified three other generic story types: comic, tragic, and romantic. *Comic* stories generate laughter, amusement, and levity with themes that might be mishaps, communication breakdowns, confusion, or, more generally, the unexpected—with the plot focus being misfortune or deserved chastisement. *Tragic* stories have a plot built around an undeserved outcome and often have a 'villain'; they lead to respect and compassion for the 'undeserving' victim and generate emotions of pity or sorrow. Many of the stories our respondents recounted about investments that did not work out were of this nature. Exhibit 4.1 also summarises the main features of the tragic story mode.

Finally, *romantic* stories have a light, sentimental quality and evoke such feelings as love, gratitude, and appreciation. In them, plots tend to focus on 'love triumphant' or misfortune conquered by love, with the protagonist now the love object. Fast Foods has some characteristics of the romantic story genre—with the business itself the love object and George Monroe (somewhat embarrassedly) infatuated with his investment. In fact, later in the interview, he became so enthusiastic about his investment in Fast Foods that he got spontaneously quite carried away:

> I go into their restaurants all the time. I stand there, and I watch. I'm, like, [asking myself], 'What are people ordering?' I was in there this morning, so—I swear to God, I was in their restaurant this morning. . . . I have a couple of things. . . . Oh, it's so gross! I was in there last night too; I got something on the train from it. They have an incredible amount of new products, and I stand there, and I watch them, and I see who's ordering what. . . . I've been in so many of these restaurants over the past month. I knew these sales numbers were going to be great because I've been, like, counting how many of these things are on the counter when I'm in there. So, it turns out one of the products that I saw over and over they even ran out of. . . . I'm not afraid to get

---

[26]Other poetic tropes used by George Monroe in his story include (i) attribution of motive (e.g., 'They [the management] really try to focus on managing their business'), (ii) attribution of causal connection (e.g., getting risk out of the business model), (iii) attribution of responsibility in terms of credit (i.e., to Monroe, who managed heroically: 'I started pushing the numbers'), and (iv) attribution of emotion ('Other people don't get so excited about . . . taking risk away').

into the trenches also and stand in a restaurant and see what they order. [And he concludes] and, so, I don't know, that worked out well, that's why it sort of worked out well.

Here, the plot relates to how the narrator's love for Fast Foods led to the recognition of special insight and understanding. Through the *attribution of emotion* (see Exhibit 4.1), George Monroe's infatuation with Fast Foods made it meaningful as a perfect investment in his eyes, and this feeling is communicated to his audience.[27] Monroe's narrative, therefore, is a story constructed around two major story types, the epic and the romantic.[28]

George Monroe's account of his Fast Foods investment shows how stories, in the sense discussed here, are powerful devices for managing meaning. They are thus likely to be an essential part of the fund manager's sense-making process and the means by which managers generate the conviction and belief to do their jobs. 'The truth of a story lies not in *the facts*, but in *the meaning*', writes Gabriel (2000), because 'if people believe a story, if the story grips them, whether events actually happened or not is irrelevant'. The keys are 'plausibility' and coherence rather than 'accuracy' (p. 4).

In our study, once we were alerted to how significant storytelling is for giving meaning and managing uncertainty and information ambiguity in the case of fund managers, we realised that this use of storytelling applied generally in financial markets, as pointed out by, for example, Fogarty and Rogers (2005). They explored financial analysts' reports and found similar processes at work. In particular, based on their analysis, they described the work of analysts as 'in its essence an interpretive or sense-making process' (p. 351). We can add that brokers, consultants, public relations firms, journalists, economists, and just about everyone else in financial markets tell stories every day.

Other stories George Monroe told, like many stories recounted by those interviewed, can be analysed by using Gabriel's four main generic story modes or such hybrid forms as the epic-comic and *tragicomic*. For example, a large number of stories were related in the tragic mode, usually in response to the request for examples of investments when things did not work out as hoped. Monroe gave one example: 'Mr Utility'.

Mr Utility was a business whose management team George Monroe clearly admired and considered to have exceptional ability. They made acquisitions, cut costs, and made these activities work, but the stock was underpriced: 'There was a valuation discrepancy between this company and most of its peers, . . . [but]

---

[27]Other poetic tropes used by George Monroe to enhance his story include attribution of credit, with Fast Foods as a *worthy* 'love object', and attribution of motive—for example, observing what people are ordering in Fast Foods restaurants as a predictor of groupwide sales numbers.

[28]It may also contain dimensions of a third, hybrid varietal, the *epic-comic* story, with the hero, George Monroe, using irony and self-insight to explain his understanding of the business: 'I'm not afraid to get into the trenches . . . and see what they order'.

that multiple disparity would eventually close.' Apparently, everything went as planned, although the gap between Mr Utility's price/earnings multiple and that of its peers never really closed. Then, within three months, the two most senior people left. Both left for better jobs, and their loss was considered to create a big risk: 'It's a fault of the board. . . . I don't at all subscribe to the notion that it's just sort of bad luck for the company.' Monroe definitely thought that the board should have prevented it from happening: 'You love this management team, you thought they would do exactly the right thing for you, you thought they would extract this value. . . . The two most senior people are both gone. . . . It just became a slow sort of mediocre kind of name. We owned a tremendous, tremendous amount of it.' And he concluded, 'And you would never imagine . . . I've never in my entire career had . . . two of the most senior executives walk out in a three-month time frame of a company that was executing brilliantly.'

George Monroe's Mr Utility story is clearly in the tragic genre, with him as protagonist in the role of undeserving victim. The two executives who let him down play the roles of villains, and the other characters—namely, the board, which should not have let these two top executives leave for other jobs—are depicted as negligent at best, if not implicitly colluding in his loss. The plot focus can be described as 'undeserved misfortune'; some of the detailed attributions (poetic tropes; see Exhibit 4.1) used in Monroe's story point to underlying explanatory meanings or motives (for example, he 'blames' the board) and implicitly 'malevolent fate'. Emotions of sorrow, anger, and pathos are clearly engendered in the storytelling in both the narrator and the listener. Essentially, Monroe suffered from a *deus ex machina* that was entirely unpredictable, and he clearly felt jilted by a management he 'loved'. Interestingly, what is overlooked in this narrative is that his thesis, that the company's valuation multiples would align with those of equivalent companies, was not working out as he expected before the departure of the executives. Monroe could prop himself up, however, with the idea that his analysis had been correct but fate had taken a hand in preventing his realising the just rewards from his work. In this way, he could avoid questioning his convictions and belief in himself.

George Monroe provided two other examples of investments in the previous 12 months with which he had been satisfied. These stories, again, illustrate poetic story modes. 'Good Foods' was a supermarket business in which he invested. At an analysts' meeting, he became interested when he noticed how confident the management seemed to be and how they sounded as if they knew what they were doing. 'So, I did more work. . . . I went out to see them [again] far away—it is one of those exhausting get up at 6 a.m., get back at 12.30 a.m. at night jobs.' He had become 'wildly intrigued', he said, and he started doing an 'incredible amount of detailed work'. The underlying story here is about how Good Foods was integrating two businesses and was able to handpick the stores it was acquiring, leading to above-industry margins. 'So, the numbers were very, very messy … and that's where … the accounting, I think, really helps my skills.' The managers also 'were sort of impressive guys who felt like they would keep their eye on the ball and keep the operation sort of running smoothly'. He was now arriving at a conclusion: 'The key was you just couldn't mess it up.' Monroe bought the stock, which subsequently went up by more than 80%.

Why didn't the other fund managers at the analysts' meeting with Good Foods pick up on the same investment opportunity? George Monroe thinks he understands:

> It's not a complex company, but people were lazy to do the work on the name, and I did it … and I did it fast. … I mean, it wasn't easy work. And it was all 100% public information, and nobody else wanted to spend the two weeks to do it. It was in the middle of August, when everyone was on vacation. … I don't know if the incentive mechanisms aren't right, … but I am glad because it gives us the opportunity to [gain] alpha for our clients.

Here, we have a hybrid story in the epic-comic genre, with a 'hero with humour' who depicts his success in terms of what he sees as his unorthodox traits, including being willing to work in the middle of August, when others are not prepared to do the hard work. The story generates feelings of pride in George Monroe's abilities and supports his conviction that his particular skills, industry, insights, and understanding are able to do what many other fund managers are not able to do. It also implicitly evokes admiration and mirth in the listener. Monroe used such poetic tropes as the attribution of *causal connection* (implicitly, the quality of his analysis drove the stock up), attribution of responsibility (clearly to his credit for getting it right), and also the attribution of *fixed qualities* (in particular, his 'selflessness'—despite it being the middle of August, he was not away but still working hard on behalf of his investors—as well as his sense of humour, imagination, and industry compared with other fund managers, who were 'lazy'). The emotional tone conveyed by the story is one of implicit criticism of other fund managers who are too selfish to do the necessary work to benefit their investors.

Another success story George Monroe told is, again, of a more conventional epic nature. This story is about 'Great Smoke' and relates to the question of when to sell a stock. The plot line is built around Monroe's ability to withstand team pressure to sell too soon: 'At that stage, everybody said, "We made our money, your thesis was right, don't you think we should sell?" and I said, "Well, let me read to you the press release and the transcript of the conference call from last quarter."' This call was between the chief financial officer (CFO) and 250 people, and the CFO said the company remained more committed than ever to creating shareholder value and had a vastly underutilised balance sheet that it was going to use for acquisitions or buybacks. Monroe stressed how, after he described the call, everyone accepted his argument that somehow the management team was going to generate value for shareholders and it was too early to sell: 'I just have to know that the management team, when I sit across the table, will create value for us. . . . They're smart guys.' Here, Monroe, as protagonist in this story, achieved victory twice—first in terms of his initial investment ('we made our money, your thesis was right') and then when he again convinced his colleagues that his analysis was right. The imagined admiration of the listener and Monroe's obvious pride in his achievement support his conviction about his abilities and success as a fund manager, which are implicitly compared with his more pedestrian colleagues (attribution of fixed qualities in juxtaposition).

The interview with George Monroe is representative of many others. Our respondents are all, in one way or another, using the medium of story to help them maintain the conviction necessary for them to engage in a dependent relationship with stocks in an uncertain world. Monroe himself is both intelligent and highly dedicated to what he does. He strives to use his training as an accountant and his willingness to undertake hard and painstaking analytical work to make what he thinks of as unemotional decisions. Nonetheless, Monroe *was* emotional when he related his investment stories. His infatuation with Fast Foods clearly came across. Also clearly revealed were his anger, still, at being let down by the management of Mr Utility and his disgust with 'lazy' fund managers in the case of Good Foods.

The emotional engagement that comes across in Monroe's interview seems to us to be a prerequisite for Monroe, as with many of our respondents, to continue to do his demanding job successfully. The power of storytelling is that it engages both the teller and the listener directly on an emotional level and by making the story 'real' and thus develops the emotional support to act. The extent of Monroe's satisfaction with, and emotional involvement in, his work comes through to the listener as Monroe became more and more excited. Significantly, in the interview, he compared himself in passing to Annie Leibovitz, the famous photographer whom he had heard speaking a couple of years before the interview. Someone had asked her, 'Why are you so good?' Monroe related how she responded to the question with the *story* of how she had been somewhere the week before with her five assistants and had said, 'Isn't this amazing!' An assistant commented, 'I don't see anything', to which she replied, 'That's why you're not me.' Monroe clearly views himself in a similar way (he was also an amateur photographer).

Meta-Narratives

The stories our respondents use to generate or support their convictions must be distinguished from what we term 'covering narratives'—that is, overall stories or, more precisely, 'meta-narratives'.[29] Understanding a bit more about how such higher-level stories are formed and structured in the investment community may thus be useful.

Meta-narratives are the narratives that fund managers—or, more generally, investment houses—use to describe their underlying investment strategy, process, or philosophy.[30] Meta-narratives are particularly suited to providing a plausible general rationale for why fund managers believe they can add value and outperform—that is, what a manager's particular competitive advantage is.[31]

George Monroe's meta-narrative is interesting. What he thinks he is doing seems to have two main components. On the one hand, he appears to believe the market is strongly influenced by emotional factors that lead to mispricing, which he can detect by using his accounting and financial analysis skills. By taking 'some of the emotion out of it', he can see through to 'true' values that others are missing. On the other hand, he also sets a lot of store by his ability to assess management quality in face-to-face meetings. His three success stories and the failure (Mr Utility) involve an attempt to reach a deep understanding of company operations and quality of management and, in so doing, to find what we might term 'unrecognised stories'. In such stories, there are exciting prospects for growth, but all the risks of what might go wrong are somehow diverted elsewhere. Monroe's stated edge, or implicit meta-narrative, is his conviction that he is more willing to do hard work and more able to keep emotion out of his decisions than those 'on the Street'. Nonetheless, as we have seen, Monroe's emotional involvement in his work and his strong feelings about his chosen stocks are apparent. Although how he expresses these characteristics is unique, the ways he uses his narratives to support himself in uncertain situations is replicated time and again throughout our sample: Fund managers both tell stories to themselves and subscribe to their meta-narratives. Being able to do so is what allows them to do their job. The key role of the meta-narrative in

---

[29]We have borrowed the term 'meta-narrative' from Lyotard (1979), who used it to mean a theory giving a comprehensive account of various social and cultural phenomena based on an appeal to universal truth or values. In this context, such a narrative legitimises power, authority, and social customs.

[30]Although we do not pursue this point further here, one can also view such meta-narratives as having a potential role in group processes—in terms of how subscribing to these common philosophies can help build strong team and house *esprit de corps* and ensure everyone is pulling in the same direction.

[31]Based on their interviews, we can state that our fund managers clearly believe in such narratives, even though their actual investment stories in many cases (as the reader will see) bear little apparent relationship to their respective meta-narratives.

assisting the fund manager's sense making—particularly when investments do not work out or the managers have to deal with the vicissitudes of the market over an extended period of time—cannot be overstated.

Although most of the fund managers rely on their meta-narratives to provide sense and structure to what they do and the stories they related, many of the narratives are rather flexible. That is, they make compelling sense only if they are not probed too deeply. This characteristic suggests the broader, symbolic purpose of the stories is to fit them to some deeper ideas about how investment decisions *are* or *ought to be* made.

What Do Success Stories Do?

The ability to tell convincing stories (to yourself as well as others) about your investments is key in generating the necessary conviction for the fund manager to enter into, and maintain, a relationship with a company and its stock. By smoothing over and creating coherence out of potentially very contradictory information, storytelling also helps anaesthetise the manager against the anxiety and stress associated with a job where investment outcomes are often unpredictable.[32] In addition, our interviews clearly show that the stock of stories of investment successes has to be continually replenished with new ones. In this way, the fund manager's confidence in his skill and ability to generate alpha on a consistent basis is continuously reinforced.

The following illustrative success stories are taken from the interviews with our other three representative respondents. In the section that follows, we discuss in detail the role storytelling plays in maintaining conviction when things do not work out.

At the time of his interview, Fred Bingham, who had been a fund manager for more than 20 years and worked for several investment houses, had been in his current position for five years. He was managing a group of private client portfolios valued at more than $500 million invested in the U.K. market. Bingham's meta-narrative is that his house has 'a stock-picking culture. . . . We try to distinguish ourselves by meeting companies. It's very vital to everything we do. It's all about meeting companies, looking at global themes, if you like, and I try to identify companies that will do well within that framework.' Although company visits are often provoked by sell-side analyst research, Bingham said, 'What we *love* to do is find an underresearched company, using our own intellectual shoe leather to find a good idea, and we look to see if the share is cheap or expensive and then go with *our conviction*' [emphasis added].

---

[32]One manager of a £4 billion global fund echoed the sentiments of many others when he explained, 'And so, if we can get 55 out of 100 decisions correct, that's pretty good. And I guess that sustains us.'

One of the four examples Fred Bingham provided of his investments that worked out is 'Amazing Glass', a U.K. engineering business that was the first company he had ever encountered when it was privately owned. The first contact occurred many years ago, and he thought then it was a 'fabulous company'. Subsequently, it was listed on the London Stock Exchange:

> The core business is toughened glass, so glass that will take a bullet.... They've got this great big cannon that goes boom, and it goes into this glass and it just folds around [it].... It's an amazing bit of technology. You'll see the American president, and he'll have a bit of [their glass] in his armoured vehicle.... So, that's their core business, which is very solid. But their real growth engine ... is the lamination of solar panels. They don't make the solar panels.... Their skill is to laminate these very brittle beasts [to make them strong].... It's a legislation-driven investment case ... also it's a green investment case. This is a proper company making proper profits with a dividend policy, and everything.... This is an undiscovered story, and we're there early.... It's a good long-term growth story.

Fred Bingham's story fits the romantic plot genre in terms of a story of 'first love'. He actually holds a large part of this business's equity: 'I've met ... the chief exec I should think about eight times now, so it's very much a two-way thing. She trusts us [that] we'll support her in good and ... well, there haven't been bad times, but we would; it's a management story. It's a good long-term growth story.... It's absolute trust about what she is going to say ... so that gives you a lot of comfort.' Here, Amazing Glass can be viewed notionally as the love object (Gabriel 2000, pp. 80, 84) with Bingham relating to it on one level as a worthy lover. He has a close relationship with the chief executive of the business, which is, seemingly, reciprocated. The poetic tropes Bingham uses in this story to generate meaning include the attribution of emotion (both loving and caring), attribution of responsibility (i.e., credit—Amazing Glass is worthy of love), and attribution of fixed qualities (including gratitude and reciprocated trust). Interestingly, however, despite his strong emotional involvement with Amazing Glass, Bingham was not explicit as to whether it had been a good investment: 'We are paying a lot, rating wise, for [their shares], but again, taking [a] three-year story, we are pretty comfortable with that.' The implication is that, in investment terms, Bingham is waiting for the story to go on and play out. His continuing excitement with his investment is clearly manifest, and this can reaffirm his belief in his abilities because of his story's face-value plausibility to him.

Mark Devreaux leads a large team running a group of value-based mutual funds and is responsible for investing $35 billion largely, but not exclusively, in the United States. His strategy is built around finding companies with low valuations that he judges to have considerable upside potential. He is also prepared to invest in distressed situations: 'We're trying to buy securities that we think are trading today at significant discounts to intrinsic value. We often look at out-of-favour names, industries, companies. So, we try to be contrarian. . . . We're striving for steady, consistent, long-term returns.' Devreaux believes that 'what makes for a good value investor is being able to, sort of, separate out the emotion'.

Mark Devreaux's meta-narrative is, 'Stocks trade . . . not always efficiently. . . . People get nervous; people get scared. And you know there is a notion of . . . "I don't want to own this; it doesn't really matter what the price is." And that is the opportunity for us, as value investors.' He said, 'And so, it's again trying to quantify that downside, trying to pierce through the smoke and the emotion and the consensus notion of "let's wait for the smoke to clear."' Presumably, Devreaux and his team can easily subscribe philosophically to this appealing and plausible narrative. The narrative is also sufficiently different from others' to appeal to the house's mutual fund investors.

Mark Devreaux described three investments with which he felt satisfied. He used his successful investment in 'Car' to illustrate to the interviewer (and implicitly, to himself) how well his investment process works. In this case, slightly more than a year before the interview, the news about the company was extremely negative, with one of its biggest suppliers seemingly at risk of bankruptcy. According to Devreaux, 'We kicked the tyres and did a lot of work. Then took a large stake'. The price rose by 50% in a short period, and Devreaux's house exited. A little later, when some more negative news hit and the price fell, his house 'reestablished the position'—a decision that he empha-sised 'was somewhat controversial. *It was not easy going against consensus senti-ment*' [emphasis added]. The stock again subsequently recovered. 'When we do it right, that's what distinguishes us', Devreaux concluded. He explained that they had thought the stock was undervalued because investors had not properly quantified the various complex risks—partly because it was not easy to do so. 'You know your head spins', he said; 'a lot of people don't go to that level of analysis.' In his assessment, the likelihood of Car actually going bankrupt was low, so the stock held 'a lot of potential upside and a very limited downside'.

Mark Devreaux's story is in characteristic epic mode, with the hero achiev-ing significant success in terms of the trial of dealing with a high-risk investment that is difficult to evaluate. He believed other investment houses had missed out on the opportunity because they had neither the same courage to take on the challenge nor, presumably, the same analytical abilities as his house has. Devreaux uses a range of poetic tropes to help generate emotional engagement in the story. These include attribution of the agency of his investment process, attribution of credit to him (and his team) for getting it right, and attribution of the fixed qualities of courage, industry, and coolness in the face of a complex and uncertain situation. His story evokes the emotions of pride in the teller and, implicitly, admiration in the listener and himself. The successful outcome also seems to provide reassurance to Devreaux that his investment process works, so he can safely continue to engage in relationships with such high-risk stocks. Also, in his storytelling, Devreaux appeared quietly satisfied with how his analysis had pushed out the emotion inherent in such an uncertain investment. His comment 'It was not easy going against consensus sentiment' suggests to him that they had a competitive advantage over others in line with his meta-narrative.

Mark Devreaux provided two other, shorter examples of similar successes. All three examples demonstrate clearly how Devreaux is able to maintain conviction that his detailed analysis and process can take the emotion out of the investment task. Cumulatively, the stories strengthen his belief in the rationale of his investment process.

Finally, let us return to Duncan Smith, first met in Chapter 2, who personally manages $18 billion in U.K. equities. His investment meta-narrative is less explicit than those of the other three fund managers. It revolves around building up 'a picture of what the market is expecting [of a stock] and where we think the market is wrong' through detailed analysis. 'It's taking an open mind—I'll look at anything—to decide where we think the market is wrong.' Smith's meta-narrative allows him to have a rationale for, in a sense, whatever he may wish to do. It is flexible. Smith's three investment decisions that satisfied him in the past year were all recounted in epic story mode (see Smith's explanation for his success in investing in Well-Managed Oil in Chapter 2).

Duncan Smith's second example is 'Lend', a specialist finance house that had been a terrible performer and that his team analyst concluded was 'a sell' rather than a 'buy'. 'But as soon as this credit crunch started in the market, they came out with a statement . . . to say, actually, this is good for us. Everybody ignored that, so I dug into it a bit more, and I thought, "I'm going to buy that."' Eventually, the analyst too changed his mind. In fact, the stock performed well indeed. Smith concluded, 'So, that was one where I was just digging around on my own, came up with the idea, and other people have eventually backed the idea. So, that's always quite satisfying.'[33]

Duncan Smith's final success story is an oil service company based in the Middle East, 'Helping Oil', which was not well researched. He met the management and was persuaded about the business outlook, so his house took 10% of the company on the IPO. Not all his colleagues listened to him. The shares then doubled in a year and a half.

In all three of his investment successes, Duncan Smith was able to demonstrate with his stories that his investment process works and he can identify situations that were missed not only by the market but also by fellow fund

---

[33]One may speculate as to what happened subsequently, after the credit crisis and the associated collapse of the debt market, to the house's investment in Lend.

managers in his house, which implicitly is important to him. These are story vignettes in an epic mode with Duncan Smith as the hero who is able to take credit for his successes through the agency of the (unique) quality of his analysis, his open-mindedness, and avoidance of emotion. His stories evoke feelings of quiet pride and serve to reinforce his conviction in what he does.

Role of Stories in Managing Disappointment

We suggest that storytelling does not merely function to generate the conviction necessary to enter into a dependent relationship with a stock and to maintain it under fire. It also plays another crucial role, already indicated by George Monroe's account of Mr Utility; storytelling has a built-in capacity to provide the means to explain and contain misfortune when things go wrong and so to sustain fund managers' morale and self-belief.

As well as being asked to provide examples of decisions with which they were satisfied, respondents were also asked to provide examples of decisions with which they were not. Among the 39 stock-picking managers (who, between them, told 165 stories about their stock-purchase decisions), 103 of the decisions eventually led to what they felt were satisfying outcomes whereas 62 did not.

Fred Bingham, whom we just met, mentioned as one of his unsatisfying examples a catering company we will call 'Burgers for Schools'. 'I got a bloody nose!' he said. Bingham's investment house had known and followed the management from a previous success story for a long time, and it was a turnaround situation. The company had a lot of debt, but Bingham trusted its management to sort this out. Then, a celebrity chef came out with a television programme that recommended the end of feeding schoolchildren burgers for lunch. According to Bingham,

> school meals didn't have burgers on the menu any more. . . . They [Burgers for Schools] did eventually go 'phut'. So, that made me sceptical, generally, about . . . how brittle this food industry is. There were other issues, obviously, and the debt was the main one, in fact, and we got it wrong. We did our analysis, trusted the management to deliver on it, and unfortunately they didn't, and we didn't get out.

Fred Bingham went on, almost in the same breath, to console himself by mentioning the stock of another food manufacturer that 'had been a big success story' and had recently been sold at a large profit. Immediately afterwards, its share price collapsed, and at the time of the interview, it was standing at not much more than 10% of the price his house had received for their shares.

Nonetheless, similar to George Monroe's story about Mr Utility, Fred Bingham's explanation of the lack of success of his Burgers for Schools investment is full of the typical characteristics of Gabriel's tragic story mode, creating feelings of, perhaps, sorrow, pity, anger, and pathos. The story also evokes some admiration for Bingham, who is able to acknowledge that he had got it 'wrong'. The plot of his story focuses to a large extent on Bingham's 'undeserved misfortune', while at the same time, the story recognises his role in the original investment decision, his mistake in trusting the firm's management, and his paying insufficient attention to the high level of debt. Notwithstanding Bingham's role, the Burgers for Schools' managers are clearly being cast in the role of villain in the story.

We think it important that Fred Bingham attributes fault to himself. In telling a story that attributes the investment outcome partly to the agency of his own investment process rather than to some malevolent fate (the celebrity chef), Bingham, like the other respondents, is protecting his underlying conviction in his meta-narrative—his ability to perform exceptionally by identifying undervalued businesses. Far from undermining his approach, he uses his Burgers for Schools experience to reinforce this conviction, even mentioning another company in the food industry where they had successfully made a lot of money. So, in Gabriel's (2000) terms, a tragic plot is now transformed into an epic one, but with Bingham as protagonist implicitly playing the role of hero who got it right. What otherwise might have been viewed as a negative story is turned into something more positive by Bingham's rationalising the fickle nature of the food business. Bingham claims he has learned something from his experiences and thus can have greater conviction in the future. His Burgers for Schools investment is not a complete loss for him.[34]

To some extent, Fred Bingham's story also has overtones of the tragicomic (Gabriel 2000, pp. 73, 85), with an 'unheroic hero' who turns out to be a victim. For Bingham, the collapse in the value of Burgers for Schools is implicitly deserved because he got his analysis wrong but also undeserved because the celebrity chef appeared out of the blue to end the practice of feeding schoolchildren burgers for lunch, which has elements of ironic humour in it. In this reading of his story, the imagined listener may not only admire Bingham for his moral courage in admitting his mistake and fortitude in getting on with the job but also be amused.

A second example Fred Bingham gave of a decision that did not work out involves an investment in 'Leave It with Us', a company that helps people after car accidents. Again, Bingham's storytelling enables him to keep his meta-narrative intact. Two other companies in the same business had done well, and according to Bingham, what happened was 'we'd picked the wrong company. . . . The theme was the right sort of idea. . . . We just got the wrong management team in place.' They went to see the company, and the management

---

[34]This behaviour is known as 'reframing' in behavioural finance. For example, advice often given to investors who are finding difficulty realising their losses is to reframe them into gains by concentrating on what they have learnt from the experience that will help them be better investors subsequently. They are also encouraged to *transfer their assets*; that is, losses are now turned into (reframed as) assets.

'had a profits warning on the [same] day', but the chief executive officer (CEO) 'didn't mention anything about it. The shares went down 20%, and I hadn't a clue.' Bingham was furious and sold out. In fact, the shares subsequently recovered. Acknowledging he had made a loss on this company, Bingham said, 'But it's what you've recycled that into' that matters, and, he added, 'Who knows? It's often better for your own peace of mind to just move on . . . and try to rectify it. Rather than having to meet people that you're not sure about anyway and not feeling very good about, just cut it and move on.'

The story has aspects of the tragic genre because it evokes feelings of anger and sorrow, but again, it also has the dimensions of a tragicomic story. Fred Bingham was let down by a CEO who, playing the role of villain to Bingham's undeserving victim, deceived him. So, Bingham is entitled to blame the CEO. At the same time, his investment process worked by correctly identifying the particular sector (Leave It with Us's two main competitors had been performing well). Also, by implicitly reframing himself into an unheroic hero ('it's what you've recycled that into'), Bingham flexibly mitigates any major effect. He demonstrates such fixed qualities in himself as fortitude, resilience, and moral courage. He substitutes hope for despair.

The final example Fred Bingham gave concerns a recent disappointment with his investment in 'Mr Sugar'. This story had been good at first; the company had been performing well. But then, Bingham said, 'They came out with an announcement that rather shocked the market, saying their sucrose business wasn't doing as well as everybody thought.' One feature of the explanatory story is that Bingham had *not* met Mr Sugar's managers but was relying on a small sell-side analyst house. Making the investment was about trusting this house, he said. 'They've got an excellent food team. . . . One trusted them completely.' On this investment and the disappointment, he said, 'Everybody got it wrong.' No one saw the announcement coming. In the circumstances, Bingham decided he would persevere with the company. 'We're not selling them.' They 'disappointed', however, and he believed, 'It'll take time for credibility to return.'

The emotional content of this story is heightened by some of the entertaining details Bingham gave of the problem that led to the announcement. Apparently, Mr Sugar's artificial sweetener worked fine in hard form but when put into fizzy drinks, which was a major growth market, changed the flavour of the drink, so Coca-Cola and PepsiCo were reluctant to use it. Such details draw the listener into the story and also show Bingham on top of the issues. Thus, Bingham's story might also be seen as more in the comic than the tragic genre. The protagonist, Bingham, is the survivor and humorist making his misfortune an occasion for wit. He is also graceful in 'forgiving' Mr Sugar's management and manifests self-possession and fortitude. Although the classical villains of the tragic story are also present in Bingham's account, he treats them much more lightly than, say, the villains in Leave It with Us; also, he was keeping his investment open and giving management a 'second chance'. That is, his investment could still play out, so in a sense he has not yet lost.

Investing in and trusting management is an integral part of Fred Bingham's investment meta-narrative. This time, he protected it by giving Mr Sugar's managers time to 'redeem' themselves for letting him down, even though the particular issues could not, except with the benefit of hindsight, be viewed as something under management's control.[35] Here, the main plot is again focused on undeserved misfortune, with its protagonist, Fred Bingham, in the role of undeserving victim let down by Mr Sugar, and also indirectly the sell-side house, whom he had trusted.

Fred Bingham is clearly able to maintain conviction in his traditional stock-picking approach and a meta-narrative that involves finding *themes* to concentrate on. He is not deflected by investments that do not work out but is able to reframe them into examples that demonstrate that his underlying thesis is sound but things cannot always be predicted (the 'malevolent fate', in story terms). Eventualities can blow him off-course. Management may let him down (the 'villain', in story terms), or his particular analysis may not have been rigorous or robust enough for success. In any case, he implies, he will learn and improve—even if how he can manage the unpredictable is left open. His stories help him make sense of his experience and generate the conviction he needs in the face of uncertainty.

For our third representative fund manager, Mark Devreaux, 'Energy', a U.S.-based coal company, is an example of an investment decision that disappointed. He bought it when news about the company was negative and a lot of shareholders were exiting. 'We did our work, you know', he said. 'Thought it was worth X, and the company proceeded to, basically, do everything wrong it possibly could—from operational issues to safety issues to a bunch of things—and the stock got clobbered. . . . [Management] did . . . things that destroyed value, and they could have taken advantage of some opportunities, but they were not quick enough.' Devreaux bought some more of the stock as it went down, however, and eventually ended up selling the stock at a significant loss. 'I bought it at X, thought it was worth, you know, 130% of X, and it got back to, you know, 85% of X.'

Mark Devreaux blamed in equal measure the company's management and his valuation work, which 'was not as robust as it should have been'. This story has some characteristics of the tragic genre, with Devreaux as the undeserving victim and Energy's management playing the villain who caused Devreaux's misfortune. Devreaux is also, however, in a subtle way, part villain and implicitly thus deserving of his fate because he helped create the permanent loss

---

[35]In fact, the idea that managers can easily disappoint investors features in many accounts in our interview narratives. It is the managers who are blamed rather than the investor because of the intrinsic lack of predictability about investment outcomes.

©2012 The Research Foundation of CFA Institute

he experienced. Emotions generated in the listener are more of pathos than of anger or sorrow. Importantly, Devreaux can find (in hindsight) plausible reasons for Energy not working out as expected; therefore, he avoids the need to question his convictions and belief in his underlying meta-narrative. Also, because his analysis is presumably under his own control, rather than controlled by external events, it can, in theory at least, be strengthened.

In a second case in which Mark Devreaux was not satisfied, 'Computers', he bought the stock as the share price was falling, but he was too early and the house experienced a 'pretty painful' downside. The analysts confirmed that their conclusion was correct, and he bought a little more; but, again, he found in retrospect that this move was too early. The stock then recovered significantly but before his house developed the confidence to add more to its position. Devreaux seemed to be most concerned that the house did not have the confidence to stick closely enough to its valuation process to add significantly to its holding when the stock continued to fall. 'When stocks are down 25%, you think, you know, "Well, did I miss something?"' His regret, in hindsight, was that he did not add more: 'I was concerned about the accuracy of our analysis, whether we really had our arms around how bad this business could get.' This story illustrates the problem of fund managers' sticking to their convictions and investment processes when the prices go against them in a major way.

Finally, let us turn back to Duncan Smith, who provided stories of unsuccessful decisions much as we have described for George Monroe, Fred Bingham, and Mark Devreaux. We discussed his investment in Outfits, the sports retailer, in Chapter 2. Smith's 'betrayal' by management lies at the heart of this plot, but this particular story can be better characterised as comic rather than tragic, with Smith playing the role of the protagonist as deserving victim or 'fool'.[36] The other characters include the CEO playing the role of a sort of 'trickster' and the CFO, an incompetent. 'From a finance director, you expect certain disciplines, and he didn't seem to have them', Smith said.

The plot of this story focuses on Duncan Smith's misfortune, which he sees as 'deserved chastisement', and the story revolves around his mistake. The poetic tropes that he uses to give the story its emotional power include, implicitly, getting his just deserts for becoming involved with this stock (he had lost more than 50% of his investment), attribution of motive in terms of how the CEO appeared to be running the company not in the shareholders' interests but as a personal plaything, and the fixed qualities of the characters in the story. These qualities include pomposity, arrogance, and vanity on the part of the trickster, in contrast to the protagonist's humility and self-chastisement. The story evokes feelings of mirth and, implicitly, scorn. Interestingly, in telling the story, Smith seems to be seeking

---

[36]See Gabriel (2000, pp. 61–63, 84) for a detailed description of the comic story genre.

to explain his investment disappointment as a particular situation relating to a founder-run business, which leaves intact his conviction and beliefs about being able to identify situations that the market is not pricing correctly.

Duncan Smith was also a buyer of 'Pharma', on the basis of his assessment of its relative valuation, its pipeline of new drugs, and the expectation that the market would soon reassess the company and its shares would go up. The general idea worked with other stocks, such as Well-Managed Oil and Lend, but over the past 12 months with Pharma, he said, 'There's been disappointment with products they've already got on the market', which had been difficult to foresee. In particular, the U.S. Food & Drug Administration (FDA) had held up approval of a key drug because of new analysis. Pharma's share price fell. 'I am no longer a buyer. . . . I just can't get excited about the stock now', Smith said. The reason? 'I got it wrong . . . because my analysis didn't highlight the risks, if you like.' The FDA delay seems to have been a stimulus to Smith to reassess Pharma's lack of earnings growth and change his view on the stock, even though he could not possibly have forecast this particular event. Although this trigger was not predictable, by viewing his analysis as faulty, Smith can retain his conviction that correct analysis would identify potentially undervalued companies. In this way, his 'tragic' story allows him to believe that the 'unpredictable' is not 'inexplicable'. On one level, he sees himself as the undeserving victim of the FDA, the villain, and the outcome is 'undeserved misfortune'.

Duncan Smith's final example of a situation that disappointed is a business he sold too soon—Special Pharma—thus missing out on considerable growth in its share price. The problem was that he never fully trusted the management, so he felt uncomfortable owning the stock:

> The goal posts seemed to move quite a lot, so we got to a valuation and I thought, 'Well, I'll take my money and run', but this kept on going up because the actual underlying business has performed pretty well and their sales growth has been better than expected.

The need to be able to trust the managers of businesses in which the interviewee invests in order to maintain conviction is illustrated in this case. He said, 'So I bought it; it went up. I sold it, but it kept going up, and it's gone up quite a bit since I sold it.' Smith's feelings can easily be imagined.

Investment Stories: An Overview

All of the individual success and disappointment stories our fund managers told are implicitly embedded in meta-narratives. These stories are used to justify, rationalise, and convince that the underlying investment processes have meaning and purpose and can lead to competitive advantage. All the stories recounted are composed of protagonists, other characters, a plot, and a predicament. The stories all use a range of poetic tropes linked together to generate emotional involvement. The emotional dimension of investment stories, as in all stories, is what endows them with truth. The fund managers' ability to tell stories, we believe, helps ensure their continuing involvement in what is a highly demanding and potentially precarious job.

When investment decisions worked out, the stories were recounted in epic (or sometimes epic-comic or romantic) mode. Here, the story is built around the fund manager/protagonist as a hero winning a noble victory in the quest for alpha, which is attributed, implicitly or explicitly, to his investment process and personal qualities and abilities. In recounting their investment successes, the managers conveyed pride in their achievements and provoked admiration in the listener.

When things went wrong, respondents dealt with the issue in a number of ways, but not by questioning their meta-narratives, the rationales behind their investment processes or strategies. They used storytelling to explain why things did not work out. Most of these stories are in a tragic genre. By generating a substantial degree of emotion in the teller (and, implicitly, in the listener), the tragedies evoke a sense of truthfulness. The plot typically revolves around the fund managers' seeking to do their job but being let down by others, which engenders feelings of sorrow, anxiety, compassion, pathos, and often, in the teller, guilt and shame. In tragic stories, the fund manager/protagonist is often a victim (deserving or undeserving) who suffers misfortune. Anger, manifested or not, thus underlay many of our fund managers' responses; they blame company managements for letting them down and also, in many cases, blame themselves. Self-blame often occurs when the interviewees feel, or at least rationalise, that their investment decision did not actually follow due process or could, with the full benefit of hindsight, be explained as inconsistent with the manager's stated investment strategy or meta-narrative. Typical story lines involve mistakes or errors of judgement. Some involve characters playing the villain, such as company managers who let the (undeserving) fund manager down. The interviewees use a rich set of poetic tropes, including malevolent fate (i.e., the sense that there was nothing else the fund manager could have done), blame (including self-blame), and the attribution of bad motives to the villain. A comparison might also be drawn between the fund manager's qualities (e.g., competence, decency, and worthiness) and the villain's (e.g., deviousness, incompetence, and meanness) viewed in juxtaposition.

In some cases, fund managers dealt with their disappointment by describing the untoward events in the tragicomic story mode. They related the stories in a humorous way that evoked emotions of amusement, pity, fear, and pathos. Here, the fund manager as protagonist refuses to give into despair but talked about his predicament in a way that makes light of it and sought to illustrate how much he has learned from his investment not working out. The humour serves to divert some of the embarrassment and implicit guilt associated with getting things wrong.

A main purpose of the individual stories our fund managers told, then, is to help generate and maintain conviction in the idea that one can earn superior returns by applying systematic and rational analysis in accordance with a sufficiently flexible meta-narrative or overarching investment 'philosophy'. Storytelling is thus an integral part of the fund manager's sense-making process. The story form helps to ensure that the unpredictable is not felt as inexplicable.

What is so noticeable in the stories of decisions that did not work out is that the underlying meta-narratives were not threatened. Fund managers use stories to interpret the adverse outcomes in ways that protect them from questioning their underlying investment processes or rationales. They explained their disappointment in terms of inadequate analysis, not holding strongly enough to their underlying process, or getting out too soon (e.g., 'capitulating' or losing their nerve). The underlying belief that it is possible to outperform is thereby left intact.

The Quant Story

Eleven of the fund managers we interviewed ran quantitative funds that used computer algorithms to select stocks for their portfolios. They rarely talked about individual stock narratives; their meta-narratives are the basis on which they generate and maintain conviction about what they do. Quants' meta-narratives are more detailed and rely on assertions about computer models being 'free of emotion' compared with the perceived emotional weaknesses of traditional stock-pickers. In this way, our quant managers see their technology and statistical processes as allowing them to analyse the enormous amount of information available electronically in an emotion-free and unbiased way, thereby giving them an investment advantage.[37]

Jeremy Swanson, who runs a $10 billion global equity quant fund, stated the argument others also clearly made. He said,

> So, rather than agonise and pore over the data of lots of different companies, we use computers to help us pick stocks. Essentially, the process is that every month, we run a bunch of programs and they more or less manage the portfolio for us. . . . There's none of the getting in at the crack of dawn to hear company announcements and worrying about the markets going up and down over the next five minutes or whatever. It's much more sort of stepping back.

---

[37]Making the claim to be free of emotion may simply emphasise just how important and feared emotion is and how the interviewees believe something has to be done to manage it. Many of our traditional stock-pickers (such as George Monroe) also create meta-narratives based on the idea that they can exploit the emotions and biases of other investors to their own benefit by debiasing themselves, even if (as with Monroe) they are nothing if not emotional when talking about their stocks.

Simon Reeves, who runs a $7 billion quantitative global growth fund, described the same idea:

> We use a gigantic stock-screening tool . . . [which screens the] financial DNA of 5,600 stocks every night. Our attitude toward this whole thing is that it's a numbers game. The process.plus us has got a strike rate of finding a stock that will beat the market of between 55% and 62%. . . . [We] never do the opposite of [our] system. . . . There is no temptation to try anything different.

Finally, 'Quintin Stevens', who also runs a large global quant fund, used an aircraft analogy to describe his role as a fund manager:

> The plane is flying itself, but there is still a pilot there . . . who basically knows how the model is constructed, knows what he is trying to do, and is basically authorising the trades as they go through. . . . So, what we do is run the optimiser, and it comes up with a list of buys and sells, . . . and [I] just work my way through the list. If you do that diligently, it's almost automatic.

The main point made by all three, as well as most of the other quant managers interviewed, is that the models they use enable them to control the biases to which they are prone. They can thus profit from the market anomalies they consider likely to result from the fact that many market participants make emotionally biased or 'irrational' decisions. In fact, their computer systems seem designed specifically to identify various market anomalies. In effect, these fund managers are pitting their 'rational', 'calm', 'systematic' approach to security valuation against the irrational market and market participants, and the quants expect to come out ahead.

Julian Edwards, for example, who runs a $6 billion quant small-cap fund, described his quant models as based on 'the field of behavioural finance' and seeks 'to exploit anomalies we witness in the financial market'. He believes that because investors are 'inherently irrational', anomalies arise that 'we can look to exploit'. He described how he can rank the desirability of the 2,000+ stocks in his universe and so take a much wider view than a 'traditional fundamental portfolio manager' who owns 100 stocks. 'Out of the 2,000 in small cap', Edwards said, 'does he really know what he doesn't own? By contrast, the nice thing is that we know about everything. . . . We have a view on everything. . . . We have a view on absolutely everything.' Leaving aside whether or not this statement is true, note its substantial emotional appeal. Edwards's meta-narrative alleviates exactly the underlying anxieties that we have seen permeate the working lives of our traditional fund managers. Computers and algorithms signify control and almost omniscience—although all our quant managers clearly realize that life is not so simple.

Meta-narratives provide the enabling story for the quants. The power and authority of sophisticated econometric models and the processing of enormous datasets provide a cloak to manage anxiety. Although the word 'science' was not used directly by any of our quant managers in this context, 'quasi-science' is clearly being used in an almost magical way to generate conviction. Julian Edwards's interview clearly illustrates this aspect. 'The hit rate . . . on an individual stock [on a traditional basis] is very low', he said. 'Maybe it's like 51%, 52%. But in aggregate, when you have breadth, all of a sudden, that portfolio-level hit rate increases significantly.' At the time of the interview, Edwards had been running his strategy for 10 years and said, 'We're talking along the lines of like an 80% portfolio [success rate] in terms of up months versus down months.' In fact, his recent performance did not differ significantly from that of his benchmark. Nonetheless, Edwards clearly gains enormous conviction from his 'quasi-scientific' investment rationale, or meta-narrative.

Although the stories the quants told do not necessarily have the same emotional charge as those that the traditional stock-pickers told about their stocks, most of our quant managers' stories are also epic ones. The underlying plot is built around the implicit or explicit achievement of the protagonist, now the quant fund manager, as hero in the quest for superior returns. In this quest, he uses the special nature and insights of his quantitative investment process. The quants use a similar range of poetic tropes to generate meaning and emotion as the stock-pickers do in the epic stories they recounted. These tropes include attribution of agency to the fund manager's statistical models and credit to the fund manager for his analytical abilities and, implicitly, his 'nobility' in not being prone to emotional bias like everyone else. Similar emotions of pride in the teller and admiration in the imagined listener are evoked in the quant interviews as with the other fund managers. In fact, almost all our quant managers became excited when they described the technical details of their systems, and they seemed as prone as the traditional managers to need plausible meta-narratives to assist them in maintaining conviction. Thus, we found the quant fund managers are also using stories to alleviate anxiety.

Summary and Conclusion

This chapter set out to explore what we were able to learn from our interviews about how fund managers are able to do their jobs when their jobs require them continuously to enter into relationships with assets (whether they selected them by traditional or other means) that can easily let them down and where the outcomes of their investment decisions are unpredictable *ex ante*. How do they develop and maintain the necessary conviction and deal with the inherent anxiety to which such uncertainty leads? We reported how our portfolio managers do what human beings always do in uncertain situations where action is necessary: tell stories.

We described some of the stories our fund managers told to support the decisions they made—both when the decisions eventually worked out and when they did not. Stories create a sense of truth by knitting various events together and evoking emotions. Their power lies in their plausibility, not necessarily their accuracy. For our respondents, storytelling maintains the conviction required to support action.

In the case of traditional stock-pickers, we found that most of the stories managers told about their investment successes are in what Gabriel (2000) defined as the epic genre, although some are of a romantic or epic-comic nature. In the stories they told about situations they had hoped would work out but did not, the typical plot has many of the well-known components of the tragic or tragicomic story genres. It is significant and interesting that because of the way the interviewees explained their failures through plausible stories, the failures do not appear to threaten the interviewees' meta-narratives or underlying investment *credos*. If anything, paradoxically, through the medium of story, our fund managers are able to use such adverse outcomes to help reinforce their beliefs in the validity of their investment strategies and processes. This conclusion has an important implication: The market as a whole, fund managers, their investment houses, and their clients may have problems learning from experience. Storytelling, in the sense we have described, is a wonderfully flexible way of explaining misfortune and managing anxiety without threatening underlying beliefs.

We also compared how the quant managers in our sample generate the necessary conviction to do their jobs the way our traditional stock-picking managers did. We found similar evidence of the key role the meta-narrative plays in providing a rationale for the managers' engagement with the market. Most of the quant meta-narratives are built around the idea that markets, and most investors, are prone to high levels of emotional and cognitive bias. The quants believe that that their dispassionate statistical models can circumvent and, in fact, exploit those biases. Supported by the recent interest in behavioural finance, such stories appear to be highly persuasive to fund managers with a quantitative or statistical orientation. The role storytelling plays in helping to provide conviction is also clear in the case of quant managers. These stories do not have the same structure in terms of a clear beginning, middle, and end from which a moral can be implied, as in a description of an individual investment decision. Nonetheless, either explicitly or implicitly, our quant respondents related their meta-narratives as if they were stories and, in virtually all cases, in epic mode. The quant fund manager is the hero, and the trial or contest he is engaged in pits him and his algorithms against other investors in the quest to generate alpha for his clients. The notional plot involves his achievement, or noble victory, as with our stock-pickers, but now, the victory comes at the portfolio level. Victory comes through the agency of the manager's highly sophisticated investment models exploiting market-pricing anomalies that arise from other investors' behavioural biases. In terms of the superior performance claimed for this approach, the narrative has an ending that is explicit (i.e., a successful outcome) or implicit (i.e., a statement that the desired outcome or positive reward must inevitably result). Feelings of excitement and pride were as present in our quant manager interviews as in our interviews with traditional managers, although the quants focused more on the 'cleverness' of their statistical models. Describing this cleverness was intended to engender feelings of admiration in the listener—presumably, the client. What came across in our interviews is how the meta-narrative that the market can be managed in this way also serves, on one level, to manage the inherent anxiety to which the quant managers are equally prone.

We hope we have provided in this chapter a theory that can help explain how fund managers of all types construct meta-narratives and stories that enable them to work at the complex and demanding task of generating value for their clients in an environment where only a loose connection exists between investment thesis and successful outcome. The use of meta-narrative and the process of storytelling provide an underlying rationale for events, and in this way, the fund managers can make sense of the world and feel that the uncertain world is more predictable. In stories, unpredictability does not imply inexplicability.

The same set of events can be explained in many ways by using different stories. In 'Telling the Investment Story: A Narrative Analysis of Shareholder Reports', Jameson (2000) took this approach in her analysis of mutual fund annual reports to shareholders. In her case, however, the focus is on reporting to investors and the ways in which the investment story is presented to persuade them that, even if their funds have underperformed in that year, their investments are being well and carefully managed. Interestingly, similar linguistic and narrative processes are used in the annual reports as are used by our fund managers. These formal narratives equally seek to engage the reader emotionally and thereby affect how he or she will respond to them. In our interviews, however, despite the presence of the 'passive' interviewer in the room, our fund managers were clearly telling stories to provide the necessary conviction to *themselves*, not to any third party.

In the next chapter, we explore what the concept of 'risk' means to our fund managers on an emotional level and how they deal with it. *Real* risk differs from the risk measures conventionally discussed in finance texts.

5. Dealing with Risk, or What Can Go Wrong

> Our institutional clients sometimes define risk as tracking error; they're look-
> ing to maximise their information ratio. Yet, you can maximise your informa-
> tion ratio and minimise your tracking error and drive your portfolio right off
> a 40% cliff. In that case, it is about *career risk*, right? . . . To me, the definition
> of 'risk' is not standard deviation, it's not volatility, it's not beta; it's what your
> risk of a meltdown [is]. What's the risk that you dig your client into a hole
> large enough that they never recover, they never get out of it? That's risk!
>
> —*Roger Sampson*

In Chapter 4, we described how the fund managers interviewed create convincing stories that generate the necessary conviction to allow them to make
investment decisions with uncertain outcomes. In this chapter, we turn our
attention to how our interviewees deal with the feelings they experience while
they wait for their investment theses to work out. Once they hold a stock,
stock-pickers enter into an implicit emotional relationship and can easily be
let down. Our particular focus will be on the inherently precarious nature of
such relationships and how the fund managers deal with this situation as new
information emerges over time.

How do our fund managers hold their nerve and not 'capitulate' when news
is adverse? How do they 'know' whether their underlying investment thesis
remains sound? In our interviews, such underlying uncertainties clearly led to
anxiety. Foreboding about future events was often bubbling under the surface.
The inherent lack of predictability and the possibility of something going wrong
that our interviewees face are the causes of concern and, therefore, might be
described as the *real risk*. This view of risk is different from the conventional
probability-based measures of risk in finance theory and the definitions of risk
used by the asset management industry for formal risk-analysis purposes.

The finance theory of textbooks represents risk statistically through a dis-
tribution of possible outcomes and thus effectively views risk as objective, quan-
tifiable, and in that sense, 'known'. In this approach, risk is typically measured
in terms of variance of returns, tracking error, value at risk (VaR), stock beta,
or a broad range of characteristic-based factors priced in the market, such as
size, growth, momentum, yield, and leverage (see, e.g., Carhart 1997). In fact,
Ricciardi (2008) listed no fewer than 63 risk categories in traditional finance.

The tacit assumption is that future risk can be estimated on the basis of past events. Lleo (2009) argued that risk can be appropriately managed through the application of sophisticated quantitative analysis and experience.

Our respondents are all familiar with the conventional measures of investment risk, of course, and these tools are used in various ways in their firms for portfolio management. The concerns of our fund managers, however, are different from these measures. In practice, what stood out when they spoke about risk was the highly emotional and visceral experience involved in being 'at risk' for making a 'mistake' or investment judgement that does not work out. Thoughts about making such decision 'errors' in an uncertain world created emotional conflict in the interviewees. The difference between investment theory about risk and real risk in the experience of fund managers is fundamental and likely to have several important implications.

Analysing our interview transcripts, we realised how our fund managers think about and deal with the possibility of their investment decisions not working out. Their concerns could be grouped under two broad headings. First, our respondents worry about the problems associated with making wrong judgements leading to *actual loss*. Second, they are concerned about wrong judgements leading to relative *underperformance*. These two issues involve slightly different kinds of event. Moreover, if a fund manager's concern is relative rather than absolute loss, the manager's concept of risk is likely to act as a constraint on behaviour that is different from the usual way risk, as it is formally conceived, acts.

We elaborate on these points by considering four specific identifiable areas of concern in terms of different imagined consequences:

- concerns about the quality of information on which managers are basing investment judgements;

- anxiety about the inherent unpredictability of what managers do and how they deal with anxiety;

- concerns about whether their clients really understand what the managers are doing and are prepared to stay the course if strategies do not work out in the short term, which constitutes business risk;

- worry about their own careers if things go wrong—that is, career risk: What is the firm's tolerance of underperformance, and how is this risk to be managed?

In the following sections, we explore what these four aspects of risk mean to our fund managers. In the final section, we describe how they apparently deal with such issues in practice.

Being at an Information Disadvantage: The Need to Be Able to Trust

The fund managers we interviewed are always clearly aware of the worrying possibility that they might not have access to the right information. Is the information accurate? Have important factors that should affect the investment decision been overlooked or misunderstood? For stock-pickers, lack of trust in company managers and what the companies are telling the interviewees is a key concern, as is the extent to which the companies can be relied on to execute their stated plans. Permeating our interview transcripts is the fear that company managers are liable to mislead fund managers—deliberately or not. As described in earlier chapters, many of the more traditional fund managers' meta-narratives involve investment processes designed to assess quality of management. 'Francine Taylor', who manages a range of mid-cap U.S. equity funds, is typical: 'And, you know, based on . . . my 18 years of experience, what's the critical important thing to me? . . . It's management quality, it's the growth prospects, it's their focus and potential to improve the return on capital.' The picture is similar for 'Mel Angel', who manages more than $10 billion in emerging market funds: 'The bottom line for us is that we believe [if] you buy good management, they should be able to manage the economic cycles as well as capitalise on the opportunities going forward.' In fact, more than 40% of the stock-pickers we interviewed (17 out of 39) directly stressed the key importance of 'making a call on management'; several stressed this point repeatedly in different ways.

The key emotion associated with the relationship of fund managers with company management is that of trust (or lack of it). Explicit references to trusting management occurred many times in our interviews. Typical are the comments made by Fred Bingham ('We would put a lot of trust in management'), 'Paul Atkinson' ('But do we trust the management?'), and Francine Taylor ('But I need a management that I can trust and believe in'). Such concerns reflect the anxiety our fund managers have regarding potential information asymmetry—that is, being at an information disadvantage compared with other market participants, including corporate executives. These anxieties are particularly poignant because most of these fund managers consider that their edge comes from some kind of superior information advantage. This advantage includes special sources of information to which they have access as well as their unique evaluation processes or investment insights. 'Morris Lawn', for example, who runs a $5 billion emerging market fund, put this belief clearly: 'We are very much stock-pickers. . . . Our competitive advantage is our proprietary research and our ability to dig down and identify what we determine is a high-quality company.'

How fund managers have to deal emotionally with the conflict of needing to trust company management while also fearing that such trust may be misplaced is well illustrated in our interviews in Chapter 4. For example, Fred Bingham, whose house, the reader will remember, has a stock-picking culture built around meeting companies, is constantly at risk of being misled by management. This situation is well illustrated in the three firms he described where things had not gone as well as he had hoped. With Burgers for Schools, Bingham put a lot of trust in its management on the basis of previous experience with them, but a TV celebrity chef talking about the poor nutrition of school food menus led to a collapse in the value of the company. Another case is the legal business Leave It with Us, which had a profit warning on the day Bingham and his colleagues visited the company; again, Bingham believes he was let down by the CEO. He evidently felt let down also by the management of Mr Sugar, with its sucrose business, although in that case, rather than selling out he gave the company management time to 'redeem' itself. In a subplot to the story, however, Bingham also felt let down by the sell-side analyst house he had relied on—'we trusted them completely'—who did not see the problem coming. In each case, Bingham had entered into an inherently precarious relationship with a company and its management. In these relationships, trusting management to deliver is key. Where this trust was thwarted, as in the case of Leave It with Us, Bingham concluded his story by saying he 'hadn't wanted to hang around anymore' and 'meet people that you're . . . not feeling very good about'. The stock ultimately recovered.

A parallel example is the case of George Monroe and Mr Utility, whose management team Monroe clearly admired, even though the multiple disparities with similar companies did not converge as Monroe was expecting. Then, the two most senior people left within three months, for which Monroe blamed the board, who, he believed, should have prevented the departures. Again, he had trusted company management that let him down.

In the case of Energy, the U.S.-based coal company, Mark Devreaux blamed management for implicitly abusing his trust in it by 'basically do[ing] everything wrong it possibly could'.

Finally, returning to Duncan Smith, remember how he described a business he sold too soon, Special Pharma: He never fully trusted the management because 'the goal posts seemed to move quite a lot', and he sold it. Although the stock continued going up, Smith had lost faith in the company's management. This story demonstrates the need of the stock-picker to continue to trust company management in order to maintain conviction. Smith could not stick with Special Pharma because 'it's checking back on what they told me the last time, and it's not always exactly the same story. So, it's nothing you can really put your finger on, but just "that's not what you told me last time."' In the case of Outfits, the sports retailer in Chapter 2, recall that the share price had halved and management treated investors arrogantly. Smith felt badly betrayed by Outfits management. He believed there was no basis of trust, that management could not be relied on, that 'the company didn't seem to care'.

To be able to invest, on the one hand, the fund manager has to be able to trust the quality of information company managers provide and their ability and willingness to deliver on what they promise. On the other hand, the fund manager always has a suspicion that he or she may be being misled. Such a dynamic inevitably leads to feelings of dependency and associated anxiety, as our interviews clearly demonstrate. Confidence is inherently fragile, and 'suffering' is an integral part of owning financial assets.

Looking generally at our interviews, we find similar issues at work. A good illustration of the precariousness of maintaining conviction, particularly in the face of adverse news, is provided by 'Andrew Smythe', who manages a $1 billion U.S. large-cap growth fund. Smythe considered 'Store', a department store with a lot of growth potential, to be 'a good story'. He said, 'We were patient with the stock . . . and owned it for seven or eight months [and then it fell a little], and I don't know exactly why. . . . [We] got frustrated with it . . . [and] just sold it.' He added, 'This was one where psychologically . . . you get tired of seeing a stock drift lower, so it's purely an emotional sale, just sold out of frustration. . . . [You wonder] "What does the Street know that we don't? What are we missing?" We just couldn't come up with an answer, so we sold.'[38] Store then went up by 50%, however, over the following six months; everything Smythe had initially identified played out. 'We just didn't give it enough time', he explained, and, interestingly, this story was told in the context of his meta-narrative of having an investment horizon of two to three years. This example shows how difficult it is to hold on to conviction under the stress of falling prices. The fund manager asks, 'Can I trust the quality of the information on which my investment is based, or am I missing out on something others know?'

Anxiety of Uncertainty

Associated with the fear of information asymmetry and the conflict between needing to depend on company management while lacking the necessary trust in it is the anxiety of, ultimately, not being able to predict the future. Fund managers are at the mercy of outcomes they could not have imagined before the events occurred. Such situations are hard to guard against or learn from, and they generate high levels of anxiety on a day-to-day basis.

---

[38]Smythe related this story with considerable emotion and evidently found the experience galling. Feelings of anger, frustration, pathos, and guilt (and possibly embarrassment for not being sufficiently 'courageous' and capitulating too quickly) were manifest. This vignette highlights the emotional pressures with which fund managers routinely have to cope.

In the previous chapter, we showed how the medium of storytelling is used by our respondents to provide plausible explanations for why investments did not work out. By believing that events can be forecast, even if one gets the predictions wrong, it is still possible to believe that uncertainties associated with the unknowable future are avoidable. In this way, the future can implicitly still be controlled. The anxiety associated with investing when there is only a loose relationship between the investment thesis and the investment outcome can be 'managed'. The conviction required to invest can be maintained.

Three of the fund managers we have described in detail in Chapter 3 provide examples of using storytelling to alleviate the tension between not being able to predict and needing to predict. First, consider Fred Bingham's examples of stock investments that did not work out as expected. Recall from Chapter 4 how he regarded a celebrity chef unexpectedly rubbishing the products of his food investment on television and the major growth area of his sugar firm facing a sudden collapse in demand as examples of where his analysis was wrong. Both cases are also, however, events that Bingham could not have predicted. By blaming the quality of his analysis, he can assuage the anxiety associated with having to acknowledge that the future is uncertain.

In the case of George Monroe, the list of areas he worried about in his interview and could not predict was a long one:

> I am worried every day. I am a worrier by nature. What's going on in the market? Food inflation . . . energy prices . . . electricity prices, the new Fed chairman is not so inclined to lower rates . . . to bail out the housing market. I think, therefore, that there are a lot of headwinds facing us.

Monroe clearly could not have predicted the sudden departure of two members of the management team of Mr Utility. 'I have never seen anything like that in my career', he commented. He was clearly emotionally hurt by this experience and blamed the board for not preventing the departures. What this example illustrates, however, is how events are inherently difficult to envisage or imagine until they happen.

Finally, in the case of Duncan Smith, he became a buyer of the company Pharma on the basis of its relative undervaluation and the pipeline of new drugs. The drug he expected to be a key driver ran into problems with the FDA, which was also slow in approving new drugs, leading to delays in Pharma products coming to market. So, the earnings outlook would now be 'pedestrian'. Smith blamed himself for getting Pharma wrong on the basis that 'my analysis didn't highlight the risks'. But, again, was it reasonable for Smith to believe he could predict uncertain future outcomes, including the results of clinical trials, except in hindsight? To believe that the future is predictable, even if mistakes are made, is to guard against the anxiety of uncertainty.

Many other respondents similarly blamed themselves for not foreseeing events that appeared to be predictable only in hindsight. Brad Johnston, who manages a $4 billion global value fund, talked about what might be termed a 'failure of imagination': He simply had not expected (and could not have predicted) something that happened. A major international bank unexpectedly put itself up for sale, leading to a sharp and sudden rise in its share price. Despite this stock's being cheap before this announcement, Johnston had not owned it because he had no confidence in its CEO. He believed the CEO was 'in the wrong business and the wrong job'. Thus, he missed out on this stock bonanza. He had a further explanation:

> There is . . . another issue. . . . I call it the C-word—the catalyst—[but] the idea that we can predict catalysts I think is [laughter] conceited in the extreme. . . . It implies predictability and a rationality that doesn't exist. . . . So, in this instance, I didn't see the catalyst; I didn't see that management would sell itself, and I am kicking myself for it.

We may speculate that, perhaps, as suggested previously, such beliefs represent an attempt to confirm that the future is controllable, even though (as Brad Johnston knows on a rational level) it is not.

Business Risk

As well as worrying about the quality of the information on which they depend and suffering the anxieties that the uncertainties in their investment task create, our fund managers also have to deal with institutional risk. This risk can be divided into two broad types, both linked with underperformance:

- business risk—that is, the danger of underperformance leading to client loss—and

- career risk—the risk of termination.

In this section, we explore how our respondents deal with the fear that their investment decisions might adversely affect the reputation and profitability of their firms. (In the next section, we deal with the risk of job loss.) What are the risks to the firm attached to underperformance, and how do our interviewees deal with these risks?

Professional fund managers recognise that it is difficult to outperform the market or peers on a consistent basis over time. Even if clients sign up for long-term performance, they often expect outperformance in the short term and may remove their funds if underperformance continues for any length of time. How do our respondents deal with this threat?

In his interview, Fred Bingham talked at length about his worries that his clients could become nervous if some of his holdings do not perform for a while (even though his mandate is to hold securities over the business cycle).

On occasion, anxieties on this score mean he has to hold some stocks he does not want because of their size in his benchmark. As a result, he feels he is somewhat constrained in making active decisions, in backing his own judgement. His worry is that clients might lose their nerve before the investment philosophy he is meant to implement (as enshrined in his mandate) has a chance to work. He plays safe because of the underlying business pressures to demonstrate short-term performance despite his long-term mandate.

A core belief among all the respondents with whom the topic was mentioned is that many clients who ask a manager to try to do exceptionally well have not emotionally agreed to the possibility that such a mandate means that the manager could do exceptionally badly. Duncan Smith is aware that clients might sign up for a particular mandate but later evaluate him on a different basis: 'The risk is if I underperform by 5%, you take your money away; if I outperform by 5%, well, you're pleased but I don't get any more money off you. . . . So, there is a business risk to underperforming.' To help deal with this risk, Smith limits how far his portfolio holdings can deviate from benchmark proportions to limit tracking error and thus the risk of underperforming relative to the benchmark. These imposed limits, of course, reduce his ability to outperform.

We observed similar business risk issues and associated anxieties with our other fund managers. 'Donald Crumb', who runs a $4 billion global fund, is unusual in that his clients are not at all interested in the short-term performance numbers. This characteristic, he hopes, will allow him to gain a competitive advantage. He can look at long-run developments and ignore the 'noise and lots of trading, lots of headlines . . . all this stuff on the TV. We call it "bubble vision." It's all too close.' Despite what he described as 'grown-up clients', however, worry is never far away for Crumb: 'You can wait a long time for these sorts of theses to play out, . . . and the market can stay irrational longer than you can stay solvent and keep your clients. But at which point would you say that a good idea is actually a bad idea?'

Another interviewee, 'Gordon Hamilton', who runs a $900 million developed market fund, made a number of interesting comments about the issue of 'managing relative risk'—that is, worrying about what others are doing and covertly matching them. For him, this practice is 'an incorrect part of our investment philosophy'. He thinks that, although the firm's managers should measure themselves against their peers, if they 'truly believed in the sort of three- to five-year intrinsic value approach' that is part of their mandate, the benchmark should not drive their investment decisions 'because you're starting at the wrong end'. This approach creates the possibility of diverging from the peer group, and he stated he does not know of 'a large investment company that can really get their arms around that' because if things do not go well short term, it would be 'such a conflicting thing'.

'Alastair Topp', who manages a $600 million global fund, is also concerned about business risk—that is, 'the risk for the fund that we do a bad job from our perspective, underperform the index and get fired'. To deal with such business risk, he said, 'We do have a mechanism around what we do to make sure we don't go too far away from the benchmark.' This is an institutionalised system of 'tracking error' and 'volatility control', as with Duncan Smith. For Topp, 'official mandates' and 'what clients expect' are two potentially different things.

'Chen Chang', who manages $3 billion of global income funds, presents a similar example of client risk. He explained that 'if the market is up 15% and we are up 12%— you know, in absolute terms, 12% is a good return—but they [the clients] would say, "Well, you're useless because you're 300 bps short of the index."' Although Chang could hold 50 stocks in his portfolio of which, in theory, none need be in the index, doing so, in reality, is 'unlikely'. He said, 'You'll get into business risk—not only client expectation, but business risk as well, and ultimately, we run a business as well.'

An illustration of how business risk can be ameliorated is provided in the interview with 'Len Williams'. He was investing $15 billion in the U.K. market with a strategy that involved low levels of trading and focused on those companies with the strongest business models. He protected himself against client conflicts by being direct about how he could not expect to outperform in exuberant markets. Moreover, because his fund was marketed as cautious and he had increased funds under management with this strategy, he seemed well placed to resist the pressure to adjust to short-term performance troughs by changing his underlying strategy. His relaxed demeanour may have been to some extent, however, because he had been lucky recently. Although generally he expected to underperform short term in 'frothy' market conditions, such as those pertaining at the time of the interview, he noted that unusual amounts of 'take-out' activity had boosted his recent figures in an unusual way.

Career Risk

As outlined in Chapter 3, another fundamental risk faced by our fund managers is career risk—that is, threats to their compensation and promotion, even the possibility of job termination, if performance is below expectations. Not all our interviewees mentioned career risk directly, perhaps because expressing such concerns may be embarrassing. Nonetheless, it was definitely present, if under the surface, in many of our interviews. Many comments were implicit or expressed in throwaway lines, nervous laughter, and the rephrasing of answers to be, perhaps, less embarrassing and more 'acceptable'. Such behaviour reveals the underlying anxiety.

Career risk is associated with business risk, of course, because if a fund manager underperforms and loses clients, the business loses revenues. And the fund manager is at risk of losing a bonus, which often accounts for 50% of take-home pay. The fund manager may even be fired. The fund manager must consider: How long will my firm allow me to underperform while continuing to manage this portfolio? Not all employers are as supportive as those of Brad Johnston, who, although he faces risks arising from failures of information, wrong analysis, and unimaginable events, does not face debilitating pressure from clients or firm colleagues.[39] The reason is that the institutional structure of his house allows such worrying times to be lived through. Johnston said, 'What would limit your life expectancy around here would actually be to run counter to what we stand for', by which he meant going against the house's stated investment process, its meta-narrative: 'If that process results in something not working out properly, then you shouldn't get too hung up on that.'

Dealing with the Possibility of Absolute Loss

The problems of what information to trust and from whom, uncertainty, and the consequences of relative underperformance in terms of business and career risk are all factors that are not well represented in standard finance theory. Fear of actually reducing client wealth and making absolute losses, which we also encountered, is conceptually a little different. Referring to the possibility of such actual loss of value, often called 'downside risk', may be closer in conception to traditional thinking. Brad Johnston put it succinctly in his interview: 'The risk of a stock falling—that's the risk I obsess about.' Our respondents described many strategies for trying to avoid such downside risk.

Mark Devreaux, who was investing in out-of-favour companies, is also aware that 'things can go wrong'. He seeks to deal with the uncertain future by trying to get the risk–reward ratio 'right'. He does so by trying 'to pierce through the smoke and emotion' to calculate the risk of loss and limit the investments to situations where he thinks the downside risk might be limited to '10% or 15% but balanced by a much bigger upside potential'. So, the analytical task is to quantify the downside: 'It is a great risk–reward for us.' His hope is that in this way, he can manage an uncertain future.

George Monroe seeks to reduce the risk of investment errors by trying to make sure he is always well informed by doing his own analysis. He concentrates on company balance sheets and looks for stocks that will do well even if only some aspects of what he is hoping come off 'because it gives you a cushion for . . . having some sort of hiccup—macro, micro, whatever'. This caution has been highly significant for him. It means that he missed World-Com and Enron. 'I never owned a share of either of these because I ploughed through the numbers.' He avoided the losses that those who held these stocks to the end suffered. On the other hand, he also missed the upside. He was not

---

[39]Although interviewed at the end of August 2007 and having a dual role as his house's banking and insurance analyst, Brad Johnston evidently did not imagine the banking crisis to come.

pleased. 'They hurt me forever.' This story highlights the significant emotional conflict between the benefits of prudently avoiding businesses that are difficult to believe in and giving up potential investment returns by not joining in while the price is climbing.[40] Nonetheless, Monroe said he continues to ask himself 'where could I be wrong', and if there is a chance of going wrong, he concludes he must 'steer clear of those'. Asked directly about what he thinks is meant by 'risk', he said, 'I'm a stock-picker. I don't know what tracking error really is.' But then he became nervous. 'I withdraw that comment', he said, 'I'm just a stock-picker, and I think about risks in the business model of any company that I own. I worry about things all the time, and I stress-test business models.' Conventional measures of investment risk, such as tracking error, are clearly not of much value to Monroe, who seeks to guard against the unknowable future by thinking about the risk of default and drawdown.

The interview with 'Mike Brown' was particularly interesting as regards risk. He works in a prestigious team with total funds under management of $50 billion and personally manages a $6 billion global fund. Here's how he responded to the question about risk:

> Well, I think people get lulled into thinking that the only risk . . . is the tracking error risk against the benchmark. But the bigger risk is the . . . volatility on the downside as opposed to . . . volatility. *Risk of loss, you know, of capital* . . . there's that element of risk as well that doesn't get fully captured in a lot of the metrics that we tend to think about. [Emphasis added.]

Mike Brown understands the danger that his investments can generate capital losses, although he thinks he is rather good at analysing when this risk is a reality and is not easily panicked by short-term events: 'My colleagues marvel at how I keep my emotions in check. . . . I try to have a clear . . . view of what the value of the company is as opposed to react[ing] to the short-term volatility.' He described how he deals with such risks by developing four scenarios for each potential investment—from everything going right to 'draconian bear'—to which his team assign probabilities 'that feed into a weighted price target, and if everyone is relatively on the same page . . . then you can make an informed decision'.[41]

Brad Johnston had the ambitious goal of finding unfashionable stocks whose value would double in five years. This he sought to do by investing in stocks 'from the cheapest quartile of the market' but avoiding 'value traps'— that is, stocks that would continue to be lowly valued. Johnston was quite clear about the biggest risk facing him—that of a stock falling long term when it

---

[40]Only with the benefit of hindsight did George Monroe know how high Enron and Worldcom would rise, and it was only supposition that if he had invested, he would have got out in time.
[41]These comments also demonstrate how the stress associated with making investment decisions may be assuaged somewhat by colleagues' having similar views.

should be rising, a risk common to every value investor. Stocks may be assigned a low valuation for good reasons, but how is it possible to know? When decisions are made to buy and hold a stock and its price stays low, at what point is it right to decide that the thesis is wrong and abandon it? As an accountant by training, Johnston tries to guard against this scenario by undertaking objective, calm, rational analysis. 'I think you can increase your chances by . . . taking a fairly commonsense, logical view of the long term, up to five years', he said.

A final illustration is William Booth, who runs a $10 billion global quantitative fund. When asked to define 'investment risk', he answered in terms of 'fat tails'—that is, the sudden impact of major shocks causing serious loss of capital—which are by nature unpredictable. 'Risk is volatility with particularly heavy emphasis on the tail events, which is drawdown, which we have all been told happens more often than the volatility suggests. That's what you should care about.' For Booth, the standard measures of risk are devices to protect managers aiming at relative performance rather than clients. 'If you have an arbitrary fund that has 5% more return than the S&P [500] but the drawdown happens at a different time, you'll get fired. So, yeah, beta risk is the closest thing to career risk I can imagine. Look, that's not real risk; don't get sucked into it. It's not risk, and it's only career risk.' When Booth was further prompted about how he defines portfolio risk, he continued, 'That's a great question. This is where I am going to go out and start fighting with the client.'

Discussion

One way of summarising the points of view we report in this chapter is to say that what we are discussing is how our fund managers, their houses, and their clients deal with the possibility that they have misread or were misled by the mass of information with which they are swamped each day. What is noise, and what is the kernel of information that has real value? The answer to this question lies at the heart of the four clusters of doubt identified in our interviewees' responses:

- doubts about the information they have and whether they can trust it,

- doubts about the unpredictability of the environment in which they operate,

- doubts about their clients' willingness to stay the course they have signed up to in their mandates if things are apparently not working out in the short term (business risk), and

- doubts about the career risk to themselves if things go wrong.

Many of our managers seem to have instituted coping behaviours to deal with these doubts. In particular, they find it difficult to treat short-term price volatility as simply noise and react with worry rather quickly if their expectations are challenged—something also suggested by the intensity and frequency of screen watching discussed in Chapter 3.

Summary and Conclusion

At the outset of this chapter, we suggested that conventional finance theory addresses what we might term 'idealised' measures of risk, not the *real* risk that our fund manager respondents experience emotionally every day. In this chapter, we showed how the dimensions of risk our interviewees are really worried about are of a different nature from conventional risk metrics, such as beta, VaR, tracking error, and volatility. The broad clusters of our respondents' concern are information asymmetry and the lack of trust it involves, the anxiety of uncertainty, client ambivalence, and career risk.

Our fund managers may rely on risk measurement models not, perhaps, for their 'truth value' but for their aid in managing a difficult set of dilemmas that create emotional conflict. Fund managers need to believe the future is predictable and that judgement errors can be minimised; also, if things go wrong, the models allow managers to avoid blaming themselves. Models, and the way in which sophisticated statistical methods can be used, may create the impression that risk can be 'managed'. Although the future is uncertain, the managers' and their clients' maintaining a strong belief (implicitly, if not explicitly) that it *is* under control seems to be important for the asset management industry.

Most of the fund managers we interviewed—for example, William Booth, Mike Brown, George Monroe, and Roger Sampson—know perfectly well that calculations of tracking error and portfolio construction using implied volatility, whatever part they play in thinking about portfolio risk, can also be used as slogans to stop thinking. As a result, managers and clients may avoid acknowledging the underlying unpredictability of future events and outcomes.

Similar processes can be observed in the production and use of hourly, daily, weekly, and monthly real-time information disseminated electronically on computer screens as described in Chapter 3. Much of this activity, it can be argued, creates the appearance of the generation of relevant information, but it actually functions to reduce anxieties about the uncertainties inherent in investing.

None of the measures of risk that are real to fund managers are measured by traditional statistical approaches. The finance literature makes little reference to the risks of information asymmetry and lack of trust in company managements, the inherently unpredictable future and anxiety this creates, or that clients often expect their managers to perform in a way different from the mandates they have agreed to. Most importantly, the literature is not helpful for understanding that the underlying visceral fear of fund managers is the risk of underperformance and career termination, which is predominantly the realm of the emotions, not rational calculus.

Although conventional risk measures are clearly of value, they do not, and perhaps ultimately cannot, address the realities of the experiences of fund managers. They may even be viewed on one level as *pseudo-defences against uncertainty*, or *real risk*. Roger Sampson's impassioned quote at the beginning of the chapter says it all.

6. Using Emotional Finance to Understand the Asset Management Industry

This book has explored the everyday world of the fund manager. In this final chapter, we draw together what we have learned from our interviews and seek to develop a research-based theory of fund managers' actual experience. Building on the evidence presented in earlier chapters, we describe how in their investment task, whether they use more traditional stock-picking or quantitative portfolio selection techniques, fund managers are essentially entering into ambivalent emotional relationships with the assets they buy, sell, and hold. In response to the question of whether it is possible to predict which investment decisions will work out *ex ante*, Mark Devreaux replied, 'You will miss most of the money to be made if you wait for everything to be clear. Once everything's clear, then it's easy, right?' This statement accurately summarises the conundrum for all our fund managers. One cannot know in advance how decisions will work out.

Everyday Financial Markets Generate Emotion

The interviews we discussed show how the day-to-day reality for fund managers is dominated not only by having to make investment decisions in a market environment of high volatility and informational ambiguity but also by the need to be special—to outperform competitors on a consistent basis. If for no other reason than that emotions are part of the evolved mental processes human beings have for managing uncertainty and competition, investment activity inevitably engages feelings and creates emotional conflict.[42]

As our earlier chapters demonstrate, the ways in which our fund managers talked about their investments, their lack of trust in their information sources and management, and their fears about losing their jobs if they perform badly made clear that they are well aware of the emotional context in which they operate. In fact, the term 'emotion' itself was volunteered freely in the interviews.[43] Words expressing such feelings as love, hate, hope, fear, worry, disappointment, and trust similarly abound in the interviews. The fund managers

---

[42]Although various distinctions may be drawn between what the terms 'feelings', 'emotions', and 'affects' can convey (Moore and Fine 1990, p. 9), we use these terms synonymously to convey subjective experience.

[43]The terms 'emotion', 'emotions', 'emotional', or 'emotionally' occur no fewer than 95 times in the 52 interview transcripts.

enter into emotionally dependent relationships with their investments that render them vulnerable and can easily lead to them being let down. Attachments to stocks are inherently precarious.

Some Core Concepts of Emotional Finance

To help us offer a coherent theory that can describe and make sense of the actuality of fund manager experience, this final chapter sets out some of the ideas underpinning *emotional finance* (Taffler and Tuckett 2007, 2010).[44] It is a theory that seeks to illuminate the day-to-day reality of investing and to apply to it a contemporary multidisciplinary perspective on human psychology and emotional experience. It is based on the psychoanalytic understanding of the human mind and dynamic emotional states explained originally by Sigmund Freud and developed by later psychoanalytic thinkers, such as Melanie Klein (e.g., 1957) and Wilfred Bion (e.g., 1970).[45]

Unconscious Conflict. The first idea from psychoanalysis that we want to introduce and consider useful is that of unconscious conflict. The idea is that thoughts always create feelings that ultimately are of two types: pleasurable (exciting) or unpleasurable (painful, anxiety generating, or loss provoking) (Freud 1911). Because many situations we face (including those in financial markets) generate both pleasurable and unpleasurable feelings, subjectively painful emotional *conflicts* are ubiquitous.[46] To avoid such painful experiences, we may use what psychoanalysts term 'defences' or 'avoidance strategies', such as *splitting* (mentally separating the good and bad feelings, with the latter being *repressed* and rendered unconscious), *projection* (unconsciously attributing unwanted feelings to others), and *denial* (disavowal or repudiation of external reality the person does not want to know about).[47] In this way, we do not address emotional conflict directly but 'sidestep' it.

Object Relationships. A second key idea is that of *object relationships*. Psychoanalysts use this phrase to describe the *relationships of attachment and attraction that we all establish in our minds with objects*—the internalised 'representations' of people, ideas, or things. We are only partly aware of this process. We tend to experience these relationships in terms of internal 'templates' based on our (unconscious) understanding of our early emotional

---

[44]Taffler and Tuckett (2010) provided an overview of this new financial theory and used it to explore a range of practical applications and market phenomena. Tuckett (2011) took a related perspective to that applied here.

[45]See Tuckett (2011, Ch. 3) for a fuller discussion of some of this theory.

[46]These conflicts also may be accompanied at times by physical discomfort; for example, back pains and headaches frequently reflect a state of anxiety caused by an unconscious conflict.

[47]For a more detailed discussion, see Moore and Fine (1990, pp. 183–184 on splitting, pp. 149–150 on projection, and pp. 50–51 on denial).

relationships—especially the feelings of desire and hatred that accompanied our experiences of satisfaction and frustration in infancy (Klein 1935). Inevitably, such relationships are *ambivalent*. Ambivalent object relationships are thus relationships in our minds with an object (as defined) in which we experience opposing feelings—typically of love and hate (attraction and repulsion)—which creates emotional conflicts. Again, we are only partly aware of this conflict.

Unconscious Phantasies. A third idea is that of *unconscious phantasies*.[48] According to psychoanalysts, phantasies are the basic building blocks of unconscious mental life and thus are deep drivers of human activity and subjective thought. They are powerful because they remain unknown and are not subject to reflective thought or conscious awareness. We can think of them as the stories (necessarily saturated with emotion) that we tell ourselves in our minds about how we relate to other people—and stories of how they relate to us, of which we have only partial knowledge. Klein (1935) suggested that the whole of an individual's psychic life is dominated by phantasies that originate in the early stages of emotional development.

The notion of the *unconscious* is not simple to explain but can be thought about as the way in which people are driven by ideas, conflicts, and feelings beyond their 'ken' or conscious awareness (see, e.g., Moore and Fine 1990, pp. 201–202). An important point to note is that individuals cannot know what their unconscious phantasies or those of others are except by inference. A good illustration is provided by George Monroe in Chapter 4. Monroe tellingly compared himself with Annie Leibovitz, the famous photographer who saw things that no one else could. In making this comparison, Monroe showed that he implicitly sees himself as exceptional, as an artist. His descriptions of how he searches out and assesses investment opportunities correspondingly cast him in the role of hero. Such ideas suggest unconscious phantasies. Although Monroe probably does not directly say that he is an artist or a hero even to himself, his selection of the example and the passion of his detailed descriptions suggest a 'half-acknowledged' underlying idea that is influential in his mind. Such half-knowing makes sense of his slight feeling of embarrassment or shame as he realised what he was revealing in the interview.

Phantastic Objects. The imagined outcomes of investing evoke excitement about gain and anxiety about possible loss. We think that, in some sense, investing includes *the unconscious hope that it may be possible to find and possess phantastic objects*. This key concept of emotional finance brings together the

---

[48]The 'ph' in the spelling is conventionally used to differentiate the concept of unconscious phantasies from 'fantasies' in the vernacular sense of consciously constructed daydreams or wishful thinking (Moore and Fine 1990, pp. 74–76).

psychoanalytic concepts of object relationships and unconscious phantasy to describe subjectively attractive 'objects'[49] that stimulate high excitement and almost automatic idealisation and, therefore, a powerful wish to possess. People imagine, although they are only partly aware of it, that phantastic objects will satisfy their deepest (and earliest infantile) desires to have exactly what they want exactly when they want it. Phantastic objects, therefore, are powerful psychological attractors acting beneath consciousness that excite phantasies of gratification or frustration. Possession of such phantastic objects allows investors unconsciously to feel omnipotent, like Aladdin, whose lamp could summon a genie, or the fictional bond trader Sherman McCoy, who felt himself to be a master of the universe (Wolfe 1987; Taffler and Tuckett 2010). Phantastic objects are exciting and transformational because they 'appear to break the usual rules of life and turn aspects of "normal" reality on its head' (Tuckett and Taffler 2008, p. 396).

Although the idea of the phantastic object originated in trying to understand investor attraction to stocks during dot-com mania (Tuckett and Taffler 2003, 2008) and other financial bubbles, we have come to think that similar unconsciously attractive notions are also at work in normal market conditions. For fund managers, who are fuelled by the pressure to be exceptional and the wish to be so in investors' subjective reality, all investments have the potential to become phantastic objects. So, investments provoke extreme emotions—with love for them potentially turning to hate and revulsion when they do not perform as expected.

States of Mind: Divided States and Integrated States. All judgements are made within states of mind. Klein's (1935) concept (later developed by Bion [1970]) described two basic mental states that oscillate. The states may be termed 'divided' and 'integrated' states of mind. The *divided state of mind* is characterised by the possession of multiple incompatible but strongly held beliefs and ideas that exist in our minds without relationship to one another.[50] Operating in such a state of mind inevitably influences one's perception of reality. This state of mind is created by the defence of splitting (mentioned above), which individuals use to put beyond awareness what they do not want to know. What is repressed and thus no longer consciously experienced, however, continues to exist 'behind the scenes', and it exerts unknown but disturbing influences. In a divided state of mind, everything is black or white; there is no uncertainty. We can think of a fund manager's emotional relationships with favoured investments moving from

---

[49]'Object' here is used in the philosophical sense of a mental representation; it could be of a person, an idea, or a thing.

[50]The correct psychoanalytic term for a divided state is the paranoid-schizoid position, but this term is highly technical and potentially misleading. These are normal states that do not connote illness. Tuckett and Taffler (2008) provided a fuller explanation of both the divided and the contrasting integrated states of mind.

idealisation (certainty) to disappointment and hatred, for example, when they let the manager down without the manager ever properly recognising that both good and bad are potentially present in any engagement with an asset.

The *integrated state of mind* is characterised by the awareness of multiple ideas linked together in some degree of coherence but not in such a way as to close off the potential presence of alternatives, especially worrying ones.[51] Here, the individual is able to bear opposing feelings and tolerate them without having to remove the potentially painful feelings their conflict creates. Ambivalence is felt and recognised, and uncertainty is accepted. The individual recognises that an asset can have both good and bad characteristics and that it can both reward us and let us down.

Tuckett and Taffler (2008) summarised the distinction between the integrated and divided senses of reality; the integrated state 'involves giving up the feeling that one is all-powerful and all-knowing' (p. 400). In the divided state, 'all such feelings are evaded by evacuating them from awareness' (p. 400). As the reader will observe, there is constant tension between investment judgements grounded in reality (made in an integrated state of mind) and those dominated by phantasy judgements made in a divided state of mind.

Groupfeel. An important concept for emotional finance is what we term 'groupfeel'. Bion (1952) distinguished between *work groups* and *basic assumption groups*, which function in quite different ways. In a work group, individuals cooperate to a common end, whereas in a basic assumption group, the members do not think for themselves but engage collectively in groupfeel (or 'groupthink'; see, e.g., Janis 1982).[52]

Groupfeel provides comfort and good feelings to group members through the unconscious defences the group as a whole adopts against anxiety rather than through working together for a common purpose. A group (whether actual or virtual) governed by groupfeel contains people who want to agree, face the world together, and be looked after. As an example, in his paper, Bion discusses the unconscious phantasy in groups that the leader will look after everyone (like a parent), so they do not need to think for themselves.[53] Operating collectively in a divided state of mind, this group's members assess information not for real thought but to promote and maintain good and excited feelings

---

[51]The correct psychoanalytic term for *integrated* state is the depressive position.

[52]We use the term 'groupfeel' here in preference to the more traditional terms of 'groupthink' or 'basic assumption group' because, although thinking and feeling are closely related notions, it is the *feelings* generated in a group that influence thoughts rather than the other way round. The interested reader is referred to Tuckett (2011, pp. 65–70) for a more detailed discussion.

[53]Bion writes: 'The first assumption is that the group exists in order to be sustained by a leader on whom it depends for nourishment, material and spiritual, and protection. This mental state I have called the basic assumption of dependence (D) and its leader the dependent leader' (1952, p. 235).

and avoid what they would rather not know. Independent thinking and evaluation is threatening, and anyone thinking differently, who might challenge these good feelings, is ostracised.

Keep in mind that members of groups do not need to be physically present in the same room for such group processes to exist; markets can also behave in similar ways and be carried away by groupfeel, with reality being denied. We suggest that groupfeel is what happens in markets when investors lose touch with thinking about adverse consequences and anxiety and get caught up with *unconscious wishful thinking*; what investors do not want to know is split off and repressed. We think this was the case, for example, with dot-com mania (see, e.g., Tuckett and Taffler 2008) and perhaps with the attractions some hedge funds have for investors (Eshraghi and Taffler 2009) and the Chinese stock market bubble (Bellotti, Taffler, and Tian 2010).

Fund Managers and Emotional Conflict

Based on the interview material presented here, we suggest it is useful to view the process of investing as one in which investors enter into ambivalent emotional attachments, whether consciously or not, with objects they hope will produce gain but which can also easily let them down and, in any case, often take time to play out. As the story plays out, the associated feelings oscillate between excitement and anxiety.

Our interviews show clearly how emotion laden fund management activity is. Indeed, many of our respondents clearly recognised this aspect. Many of the investment processes they described are designed to remove what they consider to be the debilitating effect of feelings on their judgements despite, as we have shown, such removal not being possible. For instance, George Monroe seeks to make what he thinks of as unemotional decisions by being dedicated and painstaking. Nonetheless, remember how excited he became when he talked about his infatuation with Fast Foods, his anger at being let down by the management of Mr Utility, and his obvious pride in persuading his colleagues not to sell Great Smoke. Such emotional engagement, as we have shown, is necessary for fund managers to be able to do a job for which outcomes are difficult to predict. In fact, the extent of Monroe's pride, shyness, and embarrassment when talking about his investments and discoveries was little different from how we might imagine someone might talk about the discovery of a new lover. Similarly, Fred Bingham's description of his relationship with Amazing Glass is almost in terms of a story of 'first love'. Our interviews provide many similar examples of investments being treated as love objects and their stories being related in a romantic genre. Inevitably, however, as with lovers, if things do not work out, the love can change to hate, which we saw in many instances.

Our respondents did frequently get carried away when describing their investments. In many interviews, the emotional element was evident; the respondents' language gave their underlying emotions away. To explore the nature of these feelings in more detail, we adopted a simple content-analysis approach (see, e.g., Krippendorff 2004) that counts the number of different mentions of *key words* in our interviews. **Table 6.1** provides the number of mentions of some of the emotion-laden words our respondents used to convey their feelings about their day-to-day experiences. It tells a clear story.

Table 6.1   Relative Frequency of Some Emotive Words in 52 Fund Manager Interviews

Word or Word Stem	Frequency of Mention
Worry*[a]	199
Trust*[b]	113
Hope*	102
Love*	90
Disappoint*	80
Fear*/afraid	62
Excite*	32
Hate*	26
Irrational	18
Greed*	13
Anxiety/anxious	11 (3)[c]
Anger	3

[a]Word stems include various forms of the word. For example, 'Worry*' covers 'worry' (107 mentions), 'worried' (69), 'worrying' (22), and 'worrier' (1), and 'Trust*' covers 'trust' (97 mentions), 'trusted' (8), 'trusting' (4), 'trusts' (2), 'trustworthy' (1), and 'distrust' (1).
[b]Mentions of investment trusts, bank trusts, unit trusts, etc., were omitted.
[c]Only three mentions were volunteered unprompted.

As mentioned, the term 'emotion' was used almost twice in each interview, which emphasises the essential role that emotions play in what our respondents do. Table 6.1 also suggests that fund management can be viewed in terms of pleasure versus unpleasure—feelings of trust, hope, and love (i.e., attraction) pitted against feelings of worry, disappointment, fear, and hate (i.e., repulsion). *Pleasure* words and *unpleasure* words were used almost equally in our interviews.[54]

Investing is clearly exciting. It is also anxiety generating, however, in equal, if not greater, measure. In investing, as in life generally, excitement and anxiety are two sides of the same coin. That anxiety is a key emotion experienced by our respondents is demonstrated, paradoxically, by the almost complete absence of the word itself during the interviews. In fact, Table 6.1 shows that the words 'anxious' and 'anxiety' were volunteered only on three occasions among all 52 interviews unless prompted by the interviewer. On this basis, we conclude that the feelings of anxiety that were clearly bubbling away under the surface in virtually all our interviews are difficult to acknowledge. They are repressed or evacuated from conscious awareness, making them even more powerful through being hidden. Omnipresent anxiety seems to be something that fund managers cannot afford to acknowledge.[55]

As we have seen, imagined relationships with securities are necessarily ambivalent. Insofar as the future value of assets is uncertain, owning them produces the conflicting feelings of excited attachment and potential anxiety and disappointment. Remember how George Monroe's visits to Fast Food outlets on his way to work produced both good and bad feelings, hopes and fears, depending on what he saw being ordered. Similarly, in the case of Leave It with Us, Fred Bingham experienced such emotional discomfort that he did not want to continue the relationship with its management after it let him down, so he sold out.

A key insight that we gained from our interviews is that, given the pressures on fund managers to perform, they need to believe they can find stocks that others have not already identified, with which they can have special relationships. In emotional finance terms, they are searching for phantastic objects. Although, as we have pointed out, the nature of phantastic objects is most visible in the context of asset-pricing bubbles; nonetheless, the belief that such exceptional stocks exist is also present in normal market states. Viewed through the lens of emotional finance, then, fund management may at times seem to involve a never-ending search for phantastic objects that, in unconscious phantasy, offer phenomenal returns with low or, ideally, no risk. Importantly, note that this quest, however unrealistic it is in reality, is what fund managers are implicitly expected, by their clients and employers, to be able to do. We consider this understanding important.

---

[54]The words 'trust', 'hope', and 'love' were together used a total of 385 times in our 52 interviews, or an average of 7.4 times per interview, and the words 'worry', 'disappointment', 'fear', and 'hate' were used 367 times, an average of 7.1.

[55]Although the individual *unpleasure* words in Table 6.1 reflect aspects of an anxious state of mind, anxiety itself is a far more pervasive and overwhelming feeling that, as we have shown, is often inaccessible to the conscious mind.

Fund Managers as Phantastic Objects

Asset management houses routinely promise superior returns and often advertise the past performance of selected funds to attract investment funds (see, e.g., Jain and Wu 2000), which has led to the cult of the 'star' performance fund or manager.[56] Investors tend to chase funds with high past returns (see, e.g., Bailey, Kumar and Ng 2011), even though past performance does not predict future returns, as the firms' advertisements are required to state.

As well as being required to outperform, fund managers have to carry many of the other emotional ambiguities the nature and expectations of the asset management industry creates, including the implicit denial or intolerance of the fact that the future is uncertain. The industry directly or indirectly sells the idea that its managers are able to earn superior returns on a consistent basis over time, which is what clients thus demand and believe they are signing up for in their mandates.[57] In fact, as our interviews show, fund managers themselves equally believe, at least on some level, that they are able to consistently earn superior returns.[58] We point out, however, that their high levels of anxiety suggest that, on another level, they are not so sure.[59]

Only a more or less conscious belief that phantastic objects exist sustains managers every day and makes it possible for them to believe they can repeatedly outperform others as they are required to do. The fact is that fund managers themselves are, in some sense and without deep thought, being employed as phantastic objects. They *are* the phantastic objects that their clients, employers, consultants, financial advisers, and the media unconsciously need to be superior to alleviate the anxiety they experience because of the future being unknowable. A significant consequence is that asset managers are obliged to try to *be* such phantastic objects. To be a phantastic object, a professional fund manager must invest in phantastic objects (as discussed in the previous

---

[56]Nanda, Wang, and Zheng (2004) showed that there is a significantly increased fund inflow into funds with 'stellar' performance, of the order of 13% in the following year, compared with nonstar funds. More importantly, however, new money flowing into other funds run by the same asset management house is 5% higher than funds in houses without any star funds, indicating a significant spillover effect and leading to increased profits.

[57]Outperformance is one thing; outperforming on a consistent basis is another matter. As we discussed in Chapter 3, several recent studies have demonstrated that a significant, albeit small, percentage of fund managers are able to demonstrate real skill; although as we mentioned in Chapter 3 (note 14) respective S&P benchmarks outperformed 60–80% of actively managed mutual funds over the five years to the end of 2011 depending on type. Institutional funds, however, such as pension funds, do tend to earn abnormal returns, partly because their expenses are lower (see Bauer, Cremers, and Frehen 2010).

[58]We described in Chapter 4 ways in which the fund managers were able to persuade themselves they were able to outperform, in particular by telling stories when things worked out and when they did not.

[59]They 'know but do not know'.

section)—namely, stocks that will generate high returns with low or, ideally, no risk. Fund managers have to believe that what others might view as frogs are, in fact, princes and what is perceived as base metal is really gold.

An industry that expects its foot soldiers to be phantastic objects clearly rests on problematic foundations. Reading through our interview transcripts, we see an industry built on a divided state of mind in which underlying reality (the improbability of consistently outperforming the market) is held at bay and questioning of the belief in the improbable is denied or repressed. Clients, asset management houses, commentators, and fund managers themselves are all joined together in groupfeel. Although the fund managers we interviewed are aware of the paradox we have been describing, the strength of group processes inhibits any proper examination of the paradox. In a divided state of mind, psychic excitement and short-term rewards dominate while prudence and caution are set aside. In groupfeel modality, mental conflicts between excitement and doubt are split—sidestepped or repressed—so the *pleasurable* feelings of group members are not threatened by the *unpleasurable* or painful and anxiety-generating ones. Such an unreal state of reality is hard to resist. Competitive pressures magnify rather than constrain this behaviour.

An important consequence of this kind of groupfeel in the industry is that few question whether the present structure of the asset management industry is in the best interests of clients or fund management houses. The fairly obvious divided state implied by current practices seems to pass unnoticed. The psychic excitement that accompanies a divided state of mind and the pursuit of phantastic objects is perhaps too strong and the short-term incentives too profitable for questioning the way in which the industry is currently structured.

An industry that was operating in a more integrated state of mind would have to eschew the belief in the existence of phantastic objects and clearly align the role of the fund manager with the interests of the majority of clients, who are saving for retirement. This topic is explored further in the final section of this chapter.

Being Rational and Being Realistic

What our interviews demonstrate directly is that the widely held distinction between 'rational' and 'irrational' behaviour in financial markets is not meaningful and should be abandoned. The reason is not that no irrational or overemotional investors exist or that cognitive biases are infrequent; the reason is that few investors make decisions that actually appear irrational to them at the time they are made. Certainly, none of the fund managers interviewed in our study believed they were making irrational decisions. In fact, they put a great deal of effort into collecting information, weighing and sifting it, testing for biases and errors—in short, thinking carefully about how to make the best possible decisions they could. From this point of view, they were all as rational as they could be in the situations in which they found themselves. The problem is that in a market environment characterised by uncertainty, information overload, and ambiguity, it is very difficult to act in the rational manner that standard finance and behavioural finance advocate. We need to understand how those operating in financial markets, including fund managers, actually make investment decisions and build an appropriate theory of thinking and judgement. This theory needs to take into account the evolved capacities human beings have to sense the truth of a situation and make decisions, despite incomplete information, based on cognition *and* emotion.

Bion (1962a; 1962b, pp. 42–43) developed a theory of thinking that postulates various kinds of imagined object relationships.[60] These relationships are governed by the core emotions of L (loving, attraction), H (hating, repulsion), and two states of emotional perception: K (knowing) or –K (anti-knowing). *Knowing* is characterised by curiosity and awareness, and *anti-knowing*, by the desire to avoid awareness of doubt or suspicion and fear that things might go wrong. Thinking can take place in what we have called divided states (DS) or integrated states (IS) of mind. DS is governed by –K; any thoughts that create bad feelings and thus mental pain are denied and repressed. An integrated state of mind is governed by K; good and bad feelings are equally tolerated and dealt with appropriately. This situation is represented diagrammatically in **Figure 6.1**.

This theory of thinking can be applied precisely in the fund management context. As we have seen, fund managers have to enter into highly charged and ambivalent emotional (object) relationships with stocks to be able to invest in them. They can love or hate (be attracted to or repelled by) particular securities,

Figure 6.1. Relating to a Stock: Loving, Hating, Knowing, Anti-Knowing

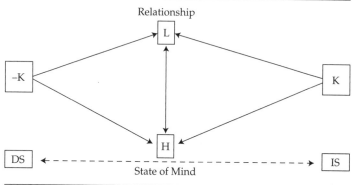

Note: L = loving, H = hating, K = knowing, –K = anti-knowing, DS = divided state of mind, and IS = integrated state of mind.

[60]Tuckett (2011, pp. 163–165) explores these ideas in detail.

but the question is whether they also *know* them; in other words, are the thoughts they bring to bear in making their investment decisions governed by K (knowledge developed in an integrated state of mind) or −K (knowledge developed in a divided state)? Real thinking includes both thoughts that are pleasurable and those that are unpleasurable, those it feels good to have and those it feels bad to have. We can be reasonably certain that any claim to make a decision on rational grounds is an indication that the issue of ambivalence has been set aside and thinking is in a divided state, probably in a group dominated by groupfeel.

Greed, Fear, and Hope

Financial markets, so we are conventionally told, are driven by the emotions of greed, fear, and hope (see, e.g., Shefrin 2002, pp. 120–121). This string of nouns is a poor description, however, of how fund managers actually operate. Although we have frequently mentioned fear and hope in this book, we have not so far discussed the emotion of greed. According to the Shorter Oxford English Dictionary (2002), greed is an 'intense or inordinate longing, esp. for wealth or food; avarice, covetous desire'. The various senses of the adverb 'greedily' include 'rapaciously'.[61] Not surprisingly, such a description did not fit any of our interviewees or their investment processes. The term was hardly mentioned in our interviews, as Table 6.1 shows.

Market participants who are dominated by greed are not really investors; they are gamblers and thieves operating in a divided state of mind without proper awareness of the consequences of their actions. Recall that Ivan Boesky, who ended up in jail for brazen insider trading and associated criminal activities, was among those who publicly advocated that greed was healthy.[62]

A far more accurate description than greed of what seems to be driving our fund managers is the quest for *excitement*, the sense of excitement or pleasure of discovering a phantastic investment opportunity (or object) that no one else knows about. Then comes the possibility of having a special and highly fulfilling relationship with it. We have given many examples of such idealised investments in earlier pages of this book.

---

[61]Klein (1957) defined greed as 'an impetuous and insatiable craving, exceeding what the subject needs and what the object is willing and able to give. . . . Its aim is destructive' (p. 181). Greed originates in the infant's desire to take as much as it wants (from the mother) with no concern for the consequences or the fate of the desired object.

[62]In a famous speech Boesky delivered on the positive aspects of greed at the University of California, Berkeley, in 1986, he said, 'I think greed is healthy; you can be greedy and still feel good about yourself.' The character Gordon Gekko in the 1987 movie *Wall Street* was, of course, based on Ivan Boesky, and Gekko's address at the Teldar Paper stockholders' meeting echoed Boesky's Berkeley speech of the previous year: 'The point is, ladies and gentlemen, greed, for lack of a better word, is good. Greed is right, greed works. . . . Greed, in all of its forms . . . has marked the upward surge of mankind.' Gekko also ended up in jail.

We also think it is useful to distinguish fear (defined as something visceral and apparent) from anxiety (defined as a more general and pervasive neurophysiological state). It was anxiety which was always bubbling under the surface of most of our interviews; conscious fear erupted more occasionally. Anxiety, as we pointed out, was rarely directly mentioned. Being repressed or hidden in this way, anxiety has an even more powerful influence on actual behaviour, because it is not 'thought'.

Hope, as we have pointed out, was mentioned frequently by our respondents. In some instances, the term seemed to be used to cover underlying feelings that things would *not* work out, almost in the sense of denial of the anxiety about an uncertain future. On some level, our fund managers 'know', but they do not 'know' or acknowledge or *want* to know or acknowledge the reality that what they are expected to do on a consistent basis is extremely difficult. Hope veils denial.

Thus, in the emotional triptych of greed, fear, and hope that is often used unthinkingly to describe investment activity, greed does not fit. We might better replace this term with *excitement* (at the prospect of gain), replace fear with *anxiety* (at the prospect of loss), and hope, perhaps, with *denial* (of ambivalence). Emotional finance thus views investors as really being driven by a specific set of excitements, anxieties, and denials. An understanding of the key role such often unconscious emotions play in all investment activity needs to be incorporated directly into any theory that sets out to understand the role of the fund manager.

Dilemma of the Fund Manager

Fund managers have to try to live up to their employers' and clients' belief in their ability to generate exceptional returns on a consistent basis, in the short as well as long term, whether or not this belief is realistic. Clearly, not all asset managers can meet this aim. As we have pointed out, such beliefs are characteristic of the process of splitting that takes place in a divided state of mind. In an industry operating in an integrated state of mind, this paradox would be properly acknowledged and the *real*, nonphantastic role of the fund manager would be formally recognised. What would that role be?

The answer goes beyond generating superior returns for clients, although professional fund managers, as a class, are able to provide better performance than what their clients, particularly retail investors, can do themselves and are also able to provide important diversification advantages. The evidence of professional fund managers' abilities to beat their benchmarks after all costs is mixed,[63] as noted previously, but a better comparison is with the abilities of their *clients* to beat the market, were they to invest on their own behalf. Unless investing for 'entertainment' (i.e., fun or gambling) (Barber and Odean

---

[63]Nonetheless, as noted in Chapter 3 (note 14), they do manifest clear skill before costs (see, e.g., Wermers, 2000).

2001; Dorn and Sengmueller 2009), the evidence is that individual investors should delegate the management of their portfolios to professional investors if they want to avoid losing significant sums of money. For example, Barber and Odean (2000) showed that the average individual investor in their sample lost 3.7% per year after costs on a fully risk-adjusted basis; the quintile of investors who traded most actively lost 10.4% per year! Similarly, Odean (1999) showed that the stocks his retail investors bought underperformed those they sold by 3.2% over the following 12 months. Barber and Odean (2011) summarised a wide range of reasons for this performance, including lack of information, cognitive biases, proneness to the disposition effect (selling winners and holding on to losers), failure to diversify,[64] and overinvestment in company stocks or the stocks most familiar to them. This type of investing made such investors feel safe, but it led to increased volatility in their portfolio returns. Poterba (2003) showed that for the largest defined-contribution plans managed by corporations, 44% of plan assets were invested in that company's stock. Such concentration is risky. For example, Enron employees had 62% of their 401(k) plan assets invested in company stock at the end of 2000; by December 2001, the company had declared bankruptcy. Not only did its employees lose their jobs, but they also lost a large fraction of their retirement income (Poterba 2003).

As many of our respondents seemed to recognise in their interviews, on one level, a fund manager's responsibility is also to manage or 'contain' client, and employer, anxiety about the difficulty of predicting future returns and the ever-present threat of drawdown. An important part of this role is to discharge such emotions and make clients and employers 'feel' better. The fund manager is the agent required to vanquish fears by demonstrating that the future is 'predictable' through the agency of the manager's abilities to outperform. Fund managers will continue to play a fundamental role in financial markets by acting as lightning conductors for their clients' (usually repressed, unconscious) anxieties about having to invest when outcomes are uncertain.

Just as the fund manager may be searching for phantastic objects, so clients and employers may need to see the manager in similar terms. There is also a parallel between the fund manager's need to trust company management, as we saw in the last chapter, and the need clients have to trust their managers. Similarly, the role of mutual trust is key in helping managers to deal with their client-related anxieties. 'It's mutual trust between a client and us', commented Fred Bingham, discussing client education.

---

[64]For example, Barber and Odean (2000) showed that, on average, the investors in their database held only four companies. Other evidence Barber and Odean (2011) quoted suggests that such retail investor portfolios are highly volatile and made up of relatively correlated securities.

Also, as anxiety drives fund managers' screen gazing, as indicated in Chapter 3, so some clients seem to require reassurance about their fund managers' ability to outperform almost on a daily basis. To quote David Allen in Chapter 3: 'We live in a world where you get measured on a daily basis, sometimes.... It affects morale; it affects your sleep, a lot of things.' And Leonard Frost said, 'Most people seem to think you can outperform not just every year but every quarter or every month, but they're living in cloud cuckoo land, these people.'

How do fund managers contain their clients' anxieties, particularly when their funds are underperforming? As we saw in Chapter 4, just as our interviewees use stories to generate the confidence necessary to make investment decisions and provide plausible explanations when things do not work out, so they use stories with their clients.[65] Jameson (2000) described how stories are used in mutual fund annual reports to shareholders to persuade them that, even if their funds have underperformed in that year, there are good reasons and their investments are, nevertheless, being properly managed. Again, anxiety is being contained by demonstrating that the unpredictable is not inexplicable. Thus, the ambivalent emotional relationship between client (and employer) and fund manager is exactly mirrored in the relationship the fund manager has with his investments.

Finally, as we have pointed out, the fund manager provides *expressive* benefits to his clients in addition to the *utilitarian* ones of conventional finance theory. In fact, Statman (2004) suggested such intangible factors as status—feeling important by association with, for example, a large well-known asset management house—patriotism, social responsibility, and fairness may even be more important to the investor than actual fund returns. People want to feel good about themselves, and an aware fund manager can help them do so.[66]

Therefore, we believe *it is not necessary for fund managers to be phantastic and operate in a divided state of mind for them to do a workmanlike and valuable job for their clients—something they are not able to do for themselves.* In an asset management industry operating in an integrated state of mind aware of the emotional conflicts inevitably present, fund managers would look after their clients' assets but in a nonphantastic way, in which the manager's task might be more successfully aligned with the client's real long-term objectives.

---

[65]Examples can be found in the section 'Managing Clients: The Role of Trust' in Chapter 3.
[66]By investing in appropriately managed mutual funds rather than index funds, investors are also able to experience 'excitement' or the chance to outperform in a relatively safe way and at low cost.

REFERENCES

Alexander, G.J., G. Cici, and S. Gibson. 2007. 'Does Motivation Matter When Assessing Trade Performance? An Analysis of Mutual Funds'. *Review of Financial Studies*, vol. 20, no. 1 (January):125–150.

Bailey, W., A. Kumar, and D. Ng. 2011. 'Behavioral Biases of Mutual Fund Investors'. *Journal of Financial Economics*, vol. 102, no. 1:1–27.

Barber, B.M., and T. Odean. 2000. 'Trading Is Hazardous to Your Wealth: The Common Stock Investment Performance of Individual Investors'. *Journal of Finance*, vol. 55, no. 2 (April):773–806.

————. 2001. 'Boys Will Be Boys: Gender, Overconfidence, and Common Stock Investment'. *Quarterly Journal of Economics*, vol. 116, no. 1 (February):261–292.

————. 2011. 'The Behavior of Individual Investors'. Working paper. Abstract available at http://ssrn.com/abstract=1872211.

Barras, L., O. Scaillet, and R. Wermers. 2010. 'False Discoveries in Mutual Fund Performance: Measuring Luck in Estimated Alphas'. *Journal of Finance*, vol. 65, no. 1 (February):179–216.

Bauer, R., M. Cremers, and R. Frehen. 2010. 'Pension Fund Performance and Costs: Small Is Beautiful'. Working paper. Abstract available at http://ssrn.com/abstract=965388.

Bellotti, X., R.J. Taffler, and L. Tian. 2010. 'Understanding the Chinese Stockmarket Bubble: The Role of Emotion'. Working paper (September). Abstract available at http://ssrn.com/abstract=1695932.

Bion, W.R. 1952. 'Group Dynamics: A Re-View'. *International Journal of Psycho-Analysis*, vol. 33:235–247.

————. 1962a. 'The Psycho-Analytic Study of Thinking'. *International Journal of Psycho-Analysis*, vol. 43:306–310.

————. 1962b. *Learning from Experience*. London: Tavistock.

————. 1970. *Attention and Interpretation: A Scientific Approach to Insight in Psycho-Analysis in Groups*. London: Tavistock.

Bogle, J.C. 2008. 'A Question So Important that It Should Be Hard to Think about Anything Else'. *Journal of Portfolio Management*, vol. 34, no. 2 (Winter):95–102.

Brandes Investment Partners. 2007. 'Death, Taxes, and Short-Term Underperformance'. Brandes Institute Research Paper No. 2007-01 (February). Abstract available at http://ssrn.com/abstract=1147124.

Brown, G., and M. Rutter. 1966. 'The Measurement of Family Activities and Relationships'. *Human Relations*, vol. 19, no. 3 (August):241–263.

Bruner, J. 2004. 'Life as Narrative'. *Social Research: An International Quarterly*, vol. 71, no. 3 (Fall):691–710.

Busse, J.A., A. Goyal, and S. Wahal. 2010. 'Performance and Persistence in Institutional Investment Management'. *Journal of Finance*, vol. 65, no. 2 (April):765–790.

Carhart, M.M. 1997. 'On Persistence in Mutual Fund Returns'. *Journal of Finance*, vol. 52, no. 1 (March):57–82.

Chen, L.-W., A.T. Adams, and R.J. Taffler. 2009. 'What Skills Do Star Fund Managers Possess?' Working paper (March). Abstract available at http://ssrn.com/abstract=1362086.

Chevalier, J., and G. Ellison. 1999. 'Career Concerns of Mutual Fund Managers'. *Quarterly Journal of Economics*, vol. 114, no. 2 (May):389–432.

Choi, D., and D. Lou. 2010. 'A Test of the Self-Serving Attribution Bias: Evidence from Mutual Funds'. Working paper (December). Abstract available at http://ssrn.com/abstract=1100786.

Cohen, R.B., C.K. Polk, and B. Silli. 2009. 'Best Ideas'. Working paper (March). Abstract available at http://ssrn.com/abstract=1364827.

Cremers, M., and A. Petajisto. 2009. 'How Active Is Your Fund Manager? A New Measure that Predicts Performance'. *Review of Financial Studies*, vol. 22, no. 9 (September):3329–3365.

Dorn, D., and P. Sengmueller. 2009. 'Trading as Entertainment'. *Management Science*, vol. 55, no. 4 (April):591–603.

Eshraghi, A., and R.J. Taffler. 2009. 'Hedge Funds and Unconscious Fantasy'. Working paper (November). Abstract available at http://ssrn.com/abstract=1522486.

Fama, E.F., and K.R. French. 2010. 'Luck versus Skill in the Cross-Section of Mutual Fund Returns'. *Journal of Finance*, vol. 65, no. 5 (October):1915–1947.

Farnsworth, H., and J. Taylor. 2006. 'Evidence on the Compensation of Portfolio Managers'. *Journal of Financial Research*, vol. 29, no. 3 (Fall):305–324.

Fogarty, T.J., and R.K. Rogers. 2005. 'Financial Analysts' Reports: An Extended Institutional Theory Evaluation'. *Accounting, Organizations and Society*, vol. 30, no. 4 (May):331–356.

Freud, S. 1911. 'Formulations on the Two Principles of Mental Functioning'. Reprinted in *The Standard Edition of the Complete Psychological Works of Sigmund Freud, Volume XII (1911-1913): The Case of Schreber, Papers on Technique and Other Works*. London: Hogarth, 1958.

Gabriel, Y. 2000. *Storytelling in Organizations: Facts, Fictions, and Fantasies.* New York: Oxford University Press.

———. 2008. *Organizing Words: A Critical Thesaurus for Social and Organization Studies.* New York: Oxford University Press.

Gaskell, G. 2000. 'Individual and Group Interviewing'. In *Qualitative Researching with Text, Image and Sound: A Practical Handbook.* Edited by Martin W. Bauer and George Gaskell. London: Sage.

Goyal, A., and S. Wahal. 2008. 'The Selection and Termination of Investment Management Firms by Plan Sponsors'. *Journal of Finance,* vol. 63, no. 4 (August):1805–1847.

Huhmann, B.A., and N. Bhattacharyya. 2005. 'Does Mutual Fund Advertising Provide Necessary Investment Information?' *International Journal of Bank Marketing,* vol. 23, no. 4:296–316.

Jain, P.C., and J. Shuang Wu. 2000. 'Truth in Mutual Fund Advertising: Evidence on Future Performance and Fund Flows'. *Journal of Finance,* vol. 55, no. 2 (April):937–958.

Jameson, D.A. 2000. 'Telling the Investment Story: A Narrative Analysis of Shareholder Reports'. *Journal of Business Communication,* vol. 37, no. 1 (January):7–38.

Janis, I.L. 1982. *Groupthink.* 2nd ed. Boston: Houghton Mifflin.

Kempf, A., S. Ruenzi, and T. Thiele. 2009. 'Employment Risk, Compensation Incentives, and Managerial Risk Taking: Evidence from the Mutual Fund Industry'. *Journal of Financial Economics,* vol. 92, no. 1 (April):92–108.

Khorana, A. 1996. 'Top Management Turnover: An Empirical Investigation of Mutual Fund Managers'. *Journal of Financial Economics,* vol. 40, no. 3 (March):403–427.

Klein, M. 1935. 'A Contribution to the Psychogenesis of Manic-Depressive States'. *International Journal of Psycho-Analysis,* vol. 16:145–174.

———. 1957. 'Envy and Gratitude'. Reprinted in *Envy and Gratitude and Other Works 1946–1963.* London: Hogarth, 1975.

Kosowski, R., A. Timmermann, R. Wermers, and H. White. 2006. 'Can Mutual Fund Manager "Stars" Really Pick Stocks? New Evidence from a Bootstrap Analysis'. *Journal of Finance,* vol. 61, no. 6 (December):2551–2595.

Krippendorff, K. 2004. *Content Analysis.* 2nd ed. Thousand Oaks, CA: Sage.

Lleo, S. 2009. 'Risk Management: A Review'. *Research Foundation Literature Review,* vol. 4, no. 1 (February):1–51.

Lyotard, J.-F. 1979. *The Postmodern Condition.* Translated by Geoff Bennington and Brian Massumi. Manchester, U.K.: Manchester University Press, 1984.

Montier, J. 2007. *Behavioural Investing: A Practitioners Guide to Applying Behavioural Finance.* Chichester, U.K.: John Wiley & Sons.

Moore, B.E., and B.D. Fine, eds. 1990. *Psychoanalytic Terms & Concepts*. New Haven, CT: Yale University Press and the American Psychoanalytic Association.

Nanda, V., Z.J. Wang, and L. Zheng. 2004. 'Family Values and the Star Phenomenon: Strategies of Mutual Fund Families'. *Review of Financial Studies*, vol. 17, no. 3 (July):667–698.

Odean, T. 1999. 'Do Investors Trade Too Much?' *American Economic Review*, vol. 89, no. 5 (December):1279–1298.

Pomorski, L. 2009. 'Acting on the Most Valuable Information: "Best Idea" Trades of Mutual Fund Managers'. Working paper (March). Abstract available at http://ssrn.com/abstract=1108186.

Poterba, J.M. 2003. 'Employer Stock and 401(k) Plans'. *American Economic Review*, vol. 93, no. 2 (May):398–404.

Ricciardi, V. 2008. 'Risk: Traditional Finance versus Behavioral Finance'. In *Handbook of Finance: Valuation, Financial Modeling and Quantitative Tools*, vol. III. Edited by Frank J. Fabozzi. Hoboken, NJ: John Wiley & Sons.

Richardson, S.A., B.S. Dohrenwend, and D. Klein. 1965. *Interviewing: Its Forms and Functions*. New York: Basic Books.

Sensoy, B.A. 2009. 'Performance Evaluation and Self-Designated Benchmark Indexes in the Mutual Fund Industry'. *Journal of Financial Economics*, vol. 92, no. 1 (April):25–39.

Shefrin, H. 2002. *Beyond Greed and Fear: Understanding Behavioral Finance and the Psychology of Investing*. New York: Oxford University Press.

Shorter Oxford English Dictionary. 2002. 5th ed. Oxford, U.K.: Oxford University Press.

Slovic, P., M. Finucane, E. Peters, and D.G. MacGregor. 2002. 'The Affect Heuristic'. In *Heuristics and Biases: The Psychology of Intuitive Judgment*. Edited by Thomas Gilovich, Dale W. Griffin, and Daniel Kahneman. New York: Cambridge University Press.

Standard & Poor's Indices versus Active Funds Scorecard, Year-End 2011. 2011. Standard & Poor's. Available at www.standardandpoors.com.

Statman, M. 2004. 'What Do Investors Want?' *Journal of Portfolio Management*, vol. 30, no. 5 (30th Anniversary):153–161.

Taffler, R.J., and D. Tuckett. 2007. 'Emotional Finance: Understanding What Drives Investors'. *Professional Investor* (Autumn):18–20.

———. 2010. 'Emotional Finance: The Role of the Unconscious in Financial Decisions'. In *Behavioral Finance: Investors, Corporations, and Markets*. Edited by H. Kent Baker and John R. Nofsinger. Hoboken, NJ: John Wiley & Sons.

Taleb, N. 2004. *Fooled by Randomness*. London: Penguin Press.

Tuckett, D. 2011. *Minding the Markets: An Emotional Finance View of Financial Instability*. Basingstoke, U.K.: Palgrave Macmillan.

Tuckett, D., and R.J. Taffler. 2003. 'Internet Stocks as "Phantastic Objects": A Psychoanalytic Interpretation of Shareholder Valuation during Dot.Com Mania'. In *Boom and Bust: The Equity Market Crisis—Lessons for Asset Managers and Their Clients*. London: European Asset Management Association.

———. 2008. 'Phantastic Objects and the Financial Market's Sense of Reality: A Psychoanalytic Contribution to the Understanding of Stock Market Instability'. *International Journal of Psycho-Analysis*, vol. 89, no. 2 (April):389–412.

Tuckett, D., M. Boulton, C. Olson, and A. Williams. 1985. *Meetings between Experts: An Approach to Sharing Ideas in Medical Consultations*. London: Tavistock.

Wermers, R. 2000. 'Mutual Fund Performance: An Empirical Decomposition into Stock-Picking Talent, Style, Transactions Costs, and Expenses'. *Journal of Finance*, vol. 55, no. 4 (August):1655–1703.

Wolfe, T. 1987. *The Bonfire of the Vanities*. New York: Bantam Books.

RESEARCH FOUNDATION
CONTRIBUTION FORM

☑ **Yes**, I want the Research Foundation to continue to fund innovative research that advances the investment management profession. Please accept my tax-deductible contribution at the following level:

Thought Leadership Circle ....US$1,000,000 or more
Named Endowment ....US$100,000 to US$999,999
Research Fellow .... US$10,000 to US$99,999
Contributing Donor .... US$1,000 to US$9,999
Friend .... Up to US$999

I would like to donate $ _____.

☐ My check is enclosed (payable to the Research Foundation of CFA Institute).
☐ I would like to donate appreciated securities (send me information).
☐ Please charge my donation to my credit card.

■ VISA ■ MC ■ Amex ■ Diners ■ Corporate ■ Personal

| | | | | | | | | | | | | | | | | |

Card Number

___/___

Expiration Date   Name on card   P L E A S E   P R I N T

☐ Corporate Card
☐ Personal Card

Signature

☐ This is a pledge. Please bill me for my donation of $ _____
☐ I would like recognition of my donation to be:

■ Individual donation ■ Corporate donation ■ Different individual

PLEASE PRINT NAME OR COMPANY NAME AS YOU WOULD LIKE IT TO APPEAR

PLEASE PRINT ☐ Mr. ☐ Mrs. ☐ Ms.   MEMBER NUMBER_____

Last Name (Family Name)   First   Middle Initial

Ti t l e

Address

City   State/Province   Countr y ZIP/Postal Code

**Please mail this completed form with your contribution to:
The Research Foundation of CFA Institute • P.O. Box 2082
Charlottesville, VA 22902-2082 USA**

For more on the Research Foundation of CFA Institute, please visit www.cfainstitute.org/about/foundation/.